MW01047546

THE LASTING WORDS OF JESUS

HOWARD W. ROBERTS

BROADMAN PRESS
Nashville, Tennessee

In appreciation for the members of
Broadview Baptist Church,
Whose emotional support and eagerness
to learn encouraged me to examine
The Lasting Words of Jesus

© Copyright 1986 ● Broadman Press

All Rights Reserved

4222-57

ISBN: 0-8054-2257-9

Dewey Decimal Classification: 232.954

Subject Heading: JESUS CHRIST—TEACHINGS

Library of Congress Catalog Number: 85-12788

Printed in the United States of America

Library of Congress Cataloging in Publication Data

Roberts, Howard W., 1947-
   The lasting words of Jesus.

   Bibliography: p.
   1. Jesus Christ—Words—Sermons. 2. Baptists—
Sermons. 3. Sermons, American.   I. Title.
BT306.R55 1986   252'.061   85-12788
ISBN 0-8054-2257-9

Contents

Contents

Acknowledgments

I acknowledge my indebtedness to many people who have made this book possible. To multitudes of unknown people throughout the centuries who gave untiring effort to preserve the words of Jesus, I am grateful. To a host of scholars through the generations who have ferreted out the best texts and interpretations of Jesus' words, I am indebted.

To the members of the community of faith whom I have been privileged to serve as pastor for more than seven years, I acknowledge my indebtedness. They have listened attentively to my ideas about Jesus' lasting words. They have dialogued and debated with me about some of my interpretations. Their interest has encouraged me to do further research and study.

To Peggy Roberts, my wife, critic, and friend, I am grateful. She was willing and eager to hear my struggles and frustrations as I attempted to give verbal expression to thoughts and concepts.

To Sandra Gardner, my secretary and friend, who helped type this manuscript, I acknowledge my indebtedness. Her insights and comments were invaluable in assisting me to write with clarity and specificity.

Introduction

The life of Jesus has intrigued me for many years. My interest in Him was kindled in my childhood home and fueled by my childhood church. As I grew older I became disturbed by some of the things Jesus said, like "Turn the other cheek," and "Would that you knew the things that make for peace." I also was troubled by explanations given as to why Jesus said and did what He did. These are some of the factors that formulated a question for me, "Why have people recorded, remembered, and studied Jesus' words?"

This question motivated me to explore what needs some of Jesus' words address. I have discovered that many of Jesus' words give expression to basic struggles I have as a human being. These struggles have often been expressed by questions like, Who am I? To whom or to what am I committed? What entices me to forfeit my commitment to God? and, What does it mean to minister to others? Jesus' words also have identified for me what is involved in the pilgrimage of faith as I seek to relate to God as Creator, Redeemer, and Sustainer of life.

Jesus' words challenge, confront, and comfort us in what it means to be human. As I have probed many of Jesus' words I have experienced Jesus' words examining me more than my examining them. You may have a similar encounter as you read what I have written. I trust your reading of this book will be a fruitful journey as you investigate with me the lasting words of Jesus.

HOWARD W. ROBERTS
BROADVIEW BAPTIST CHURCH
TEMPLE HILLS, MARYLAND

1

The Searching Words of Jesus
Luke 2:41-52

Have you ever prefaced an inquiry with the qualifier, "I know this is a dumb question"? Actually, the only dumb question is the unasked one. Curiosity and inquisitiveness are signs of a fertile mind from which sprouts concepts, ideas, and visions. Unless the questions are formulated and expressed, the visions do not germinate and actions are not taken to give expression to the questioner's interior life.

Jesus' Temple Visit

The words in Luke's Gospel (Luke 2:41-52) record the first statement attributed to Jesus in the New Testament. Certainly Jesus was not mute the first eleven years of His life. There is every reason to believe He made himself known when He was presented in the Temple the eighth day after his birth. I have yet to have an infant presented at the time of parent-child dedication when the child did not make his presence known with a coo, a cry, or both.

Luke is the only author who included in his writings the presentation of the infant Jesus in the Temple and Jesus' first visit to the Temple at age twelve. In a matter-of-fact style, Luke wrote that every year Joseph and Mary walked the seventy miles from Nazareth to Jerusalem to celebrate Passover. Fulfillment of the religious law required every Jewish adult male to participate in the feasts of Passover, Pentecost, and Tabernacles, but many Jews who lived after the Exile found it impossible to keep this law because of the distance between their homes and Jerusalem.

The residents of Palestine did make a concerted effort to be in Jerusalem for at least one of the feasts each year, and Passover was, by far, the most popular of the three. Although women were not bound by this law, many of them did accompany male family members on these pilgrimages. Luke underscored the devoutness of Joseph and Mary by stating that they celebrated Passover in Jerusalem every year. According to the law, the Feast of Unleavened bread followed the Passover celebration immediately and was observed for seven days (Ex. 23:15). Participation in the Passover celebration required only two days, after which many of the pilgrims began their treks home.

As Luke told it, when Jesus was twelve He went with his parents to Jerusalem to celebrate Passover. Apparently, the first eleven years Jesus stayed with friends or family while Joseph and Mary made their pilgrimage, but the twelfth year was different. It was at age twelve that a boy became a man with regard to the moral, ethical, and religious laws. From his twelfth birthday, a Jewish boy was identified as a son of the law. In many ways, age twelve was in Jesus' culture what age eighteen is in ours.

Why was Luke, a Gentile, the only biblical writer to include the first Temple visit in his account of Jesus' life? Could it be that the other writers saw nothing unusual about a custom with which they were very familiar? Of course, each Gospel writer had his own purposes and audience in mind. It also is accepted by many that Mary was one of Luke's primary eyewitnesses. Perhaps Luke was captivated by the emotion with which Mary told this incident. Luke also may have wanted to demonstrate very early some attributes of Jesus' nature. Jesus is forever pictured as a Question Man, although many, then and now, want Him to be an Answer Man. Certainly, this event reveals Jesus searching and questioning as one thirsty for knowledge and understanding.

Can you imagine the excitement Jesus felt going to the Temple in Jerusalem? For several years He had seen his parents off to Jerusalem and sensed the excitement of the caravan of pilgrims as they renewed acquaintances and swapped recollections. For the previous two or three years He had probably longed to go with them, wanting to be part of the crowd of pilgrims, wanting to see Jerusalem and the Temple, wanting to hear the stories firsthand rather than warmed over, wondering what it would be like to hike for a week and camp out overnight. He knew about Passover and had celebrated the feast many times in Nazareth, but Nazareth wasn't Jerusalem, and it had not been with His parents. Jerusalem was the city of His dreams.

In addition to all of this, to go to Jerusalem would make a statement about Him. It would say He was growing up. He had seen all of the attention that older boys had received when they returned from Jerusalem. It seemed that after His older friends returned from Jerusalem they were included with the adults in discussions and decisions that affected them. To go to Jerusalem was a routine trip for those who went every year, but for Jesus, going to Jerusalem for the first time was one giant, life-changing event. It was a time when family, friends, casual acquaintances, and even those who didn't know Jesus acknowledged that He was becoming a man, a son of the law. His feet probably only touched the ground a time or two during the entire seventy-mile walk. The rocks along the way could not have been more beautiful. The desert flowers could not have been brighter or the Palestinian sky bluer.

As the caravan crested the hill near Jerusalem, there was the Temple in all its radiant splendor. Some of the Temple was decorated with gold, so that when the sunlight poured upon it, the shining reflection caused people to turn away their eyes like they would turn them from the brightness of the sun. As Jesus drew closer to the Temple, He joined His voice with fellow pilgrims in singing, "I was glad when they said to me, 'Let us go into the house of the Lord' " (Ps. 122:1).

Jesus had expected the Temple to be beautiful, and it was, even more than He had imagined. He had not seen in His mind the radiant splendor caused by the gold reflecting the sun's rays. The city of Jerusalem was just as Jesus had expected, even better. He was overwhelmed at the crowds of people. They were excited and exciting! Everyone was so friendly. Even strangers spoke to Him and showed genuine interest in Him, congratulating Him on celebrating His first Passover in Jerusalem. All of this happened before He came near the Temple and before the Passover celebration even began. Jesus wondered if He would be able to absorb it all. The most minute incident suddenly took on the grandeur of importance. Wide-eyed, he drank in the beauty and the heritage of the Temple. With pounding eardrums He heard sounds and voices that were feverish with excitement.

Significant to the Passover celebration was the preparation of the paschal lamb for each family. The Passover lambs were killed on the afternoon preceding the day of the Passover meal. The lamb was a sacrifice that had to be killed in the Temple courtyard. The blood of the animal was given to God. Blood was identified with the life of the animal, and life belonged to God, the Creator of life. At His first Passover in Jerusalem, Jesus went with Joseph to kill a lamb and to offer its blood to God. They took their place in the long line of men waiting to kill their sacrificial lambs. At last their turn came. Priests were there to assist as they slit the throat of their lamb. A priest caught the blood in a basin, passed the blood to another priest, and he to another. The priest nearest the altar tossed the blood against the base of the altar.[1]

Surely the radiant splendor of the Temple that Jesus had seen earlier as He crested the hill outside Jerusalem was tainted, if not lost completely, by the slaughterhouse odor of the Temple courtyard. It is doubtful that anyone had warned Jesus about this aspect of Passover. As with most festivities, people tend to talk about the beauty and excitement and leave out the details of preparation and strange or foul sights, sounds, or odors. For a boy experiencing Passover in Jerusalem for the first time, the slaughtering of lambs in the courtyard must have been as shocking as His first glimpse of the Temple was awesome.

Jesus' Education in the Temple

In the synagogue in Nazareth Jesus had heard about the learned men of the Sanhedrin who discussed the matters of religion and its application to life. Normally, they met behind closed doors except at Passover, when they met in public and invited to their discussions any who wanted to listen. One of the plans Jesus made before He even left Nazareth was to listen to the Sanhedrin discussions. The day after the Passover meal, Jesus found the teachers in the courtyard with many eager learners sitting at their feet. He inched His way toward the group until He was within earshot. As He listened, He edged His way closer and closer. Eventually He was sitting at the feet of the teachers, enthralled with what they were saying, engaged in dialogue, asking questions, having no idea what time it was, and thinking deeply, but not about His parents. The first words spoken by Jesus recorded in the New Testament are set in the context of Jesus listening to and asking questions of the teachers in the Temple.

Have you ever wondered what questions Jesus asked the Sanhedrin? The questions a person asks reveal a great deal about him. They indicate personal interests, inquisitiveness, curiosity, insight, and knowledge. I suspect that these characteristics were revealed about Jesus through His questions of the Sanhedrin. There may have been some who marveled that one so young not only would show such interest in religious matters but also was at ease enough to engage the teachers in dialogue, listening to them, and asking them questions.

Apparently Jesus' interest and questions absorbed His attention. This could partially explain how Jesus became separated from His parents. With so many people around, it easily could have happened. Perhaps Joseph thought Jesus was with Mary, and Mary thought He was with Joseph. Sometimes family members did not get together until evening, so there would have been no concern about Jesus' whereabouts during the day.

Jesus' Separation from Joseph and Mary

Once Joseph and Mary learned that Jesus was missing, it was evening. They could not begin their search until the next morning. What a long, restless night that must have been! They thought dawn would never arrive. When it did, there was the calmness that came with being able to do something rather than just wait. Joseph and Mary began to backtrack the previous day's journey, leaving no bush unseen, no ditch unsearched, no hill unscaled. They tried to remember what He had been wearing and attempted to describe Him to anyone they met. Every traveler they saw caused hope to rise in them that the traveler had seen Jesus and could tell them where He was. But nobody had seen Him.

Tremendous anguish is experienced in searching for a missing child. While my family was on vacation in 1982, we took a delightful and exhilarating hike in the woods. As we neared the end of the trail, Melanie and Danita, who were ten and seven, went on ahead and were to meet us at our cabin. When we arrived at the cabin, neither of the girls was in sight or sound. I have no idea how many times I called their names. I walked the terrain many times. I tried to anticipate which direction they had gone. I was astonished at how many lives I lived, how much sadness I felt, the fear I experienced, the emotional bruises I inflicted upon myself, and the regrets I listed. All of this occurred in two hours—120 long minutes. And oh, what joyful relief was mine when the park police brought Melanie and Danita to the door.

For Joseph and Mary, the agony lasted two nights and a day. The first day they didn't know Jesus was gone, and the third day they found Him. Finally, relief came for Joseph and Mary when they arrived in the Temple courtyard. Luke said they were astonished when they saw Jesus. Perhaps they had begun to tell themselves they weren't going to find Him. Surely by now, if He were safe, He would be searching for them! They could think of no reason why Jesus would still be in the Temple, but they had looked everywhere else. They decided at least to ask some of the priests if they had seen Him. And there He was—listening and questioning the religion professors.

Mary did not verbalize her feelings of relief and astonishment that Jesus had been found. Rather, she expressed her anger at Him for treating her and Joseph so unthinkingly. Isn't Mary's response characteristic of a parent? Whenever we have made a mistake or at least bear some responsibility for things having gone badly with our children, we quickly point out what the child did wrong or where she failed to act according to our expectations. Part of our rationale for projecting our frustrations onto our children is our anxiety that someone would see a parental mistake as neglect or failure to be good parents. We react defensively and angrily.

Winston Churchill told the story of a man who risked his life to save a child from drowning and delivered the child, all but his clothes intact, to his mother. Whereupon the mother merely snapped the question, "Where's Johnny's cap?" Probably she was beating herself up inside, saying, "I can't believe I was so irresponsible as to let Johnny nearly drown. Now this man knows what a terrible mother I am. I'm afraid to talk to him. He will just condemn me. I'm already so vulnerable, I can't let him get close to me. I'll keep him at a distance by pointing out a weakness in him. He thinks he's done a great job saving Johnny, but he could have done better. He lost Johnny's cap."

Mary reacted in a similar way when she found Jesus. Nearly thirteen years earlier when the heavenly messenger told her about her pregnancy, nothing was said about the agony and frustration she would feel when she did not know where her son was. Perhaps part of her frustration came from her concern about what others would think about her. After all, this boy had been there three days with no parents in sight. What kind of parents would just leave Him there with no provision for food or shelter? After all of the searching and the hours of agony, upon seeing Jesus, Mary blurted out, "Son, why have you treated us so? Behold your father and I have been looking for you anxiously" (Luke 2:48). Whenever children do not act according to their parents' expectations, there often is disappointment and hurt. Some parents, like Mary, conclude that children plot to do in the parents. Encouraging children to think for themselves is risky, because they will not always think like their parents. This is illustrated with Joseph, Mary, and Jesus in this incident.

Evidence of Jesus' Growth

Jesus' response to Mary's question is directed to both Mary and

Joseph, and it is quite surprising. One would expect Jesus to respond in kind to Mary and Joseph. He could have said, "Mother, Dad, why have you treated Me this way? I had no place to eat and nowhere to sleep? Where have you been? Why did you leave without telling Me you were going?" Jesus could have exploited the guilt Mary felt for having left Him by telling her how frightened He had been and how He had wondered several times if He would ever see His parents again. He could have used this event to distance Himself from them by arrogantly retorting, "Well, I'm old enough to take care of Myself. I'm capable of making My own decisions, and one of those decisions was to stay here at the Temple for awhile and learn. I'm surprised you didn't stay, as religious as you are and as many questions you claim to have about religious matters."

Jesus' answer was surprising because He was surprised. He was surprised that they had been looking for Him. He had been a responsible person for a long time. Perhaps they had commented on that many times. His parents may have known of His interest in listening to the teachers. That had been one of His interests in making His first pilgrimage to Jerusalem. So why had they panicked and gone off searching for Him as if He were lost? Where did they think He would be, if not in the Temple?

Part of the surprise for Jesus also may have resulted from His becoming aware that Joseph and Mary knew nothing of His personal and private intuitions that had been running through His mind at different times. It is not too unusual for a person to think about some things either so clearly or so often, or both, that because they are common in his thinking, he assumes those around him, especially those closest to him, think exactly as he thinks and feel like he feels.

I recall diligently saving money for college throughout my high school years, fully expecting to be required to pay for a large portion of my college education myself. I thought about this so often that I assumed my parents thought the same thing. I can still feel the elated surprise I experienced just after high school graduation when my dad told me that he had planned to pay for my college education. He insisted on it and encouraged me to use my savings in some other way. I suddenly was aware that my thoughts had not been my dad's thoughts.

This type of dynamic was part of the surprise for Jesus when His parents found Him and were amazed both that they found Him and where He was. In the language of transactional analysis, the possible responses mentioned in the previous paragraphs were either parent or child responses. Those responses would either have continued the destructive communication pattern begun by Mary with her question, "Why have you treated us so?" or they would have moved the communication pattern in another destructive direction. Jesus could have been parental by asking, "Where have you been? Why did you leave me without telling me where you were going?" There is evidence that Jesus was tempted to respond in one of these ways. The writer of Hebrews says that He was tempted in every way as we are (Heb. 4:15).

Whenever a communication pattern is in a destructive mode, one of the persons involved must make a conscious decision to relate and communicate in a more wholesome way or the communication, and eventually the entire relationship, will become destructive and disintegrate. One helpful method to break out of a destructive communication pattern is for one person to respond in an unexpected way. If two children are fighting and one of them says, "If you hit me again, I'm going to kiss you," the one hitting is so surprised that he halts his hitting at least long enough to chuckle, which is enough time to shift the communication pattern in a positive direction. Jesus took this approach in His ministry when He taught to return good for evil because to return evil for evil only increased the evil in the world.

Jesus took a step toward returning good for evil in His first dialogue recorded in Scripture. Jesus' question to Joseph and Mary, "Did you not know that I would be involved in My Father's affairs?" Luke 2:49, author's translation). was not the response either of them expected. What response did they expect? They may have expected, "I'm sorry," "Why are you yelling at Me?" "Why are you blaming Me?" or "Where have you been?" Jesus' response surprised them because His response involved self-direction and the ability to move out and meet life.

The question Jesus asked Joseph and Mary was a lasting word because it dealt with the perennial issue of temptation. He was tempted to be either compliant or defiant. Jesus could have been compliant and simply caved in to the emotional avalanche He received from Mary. He could have said, "You are right. I should not have stayed listening and questioning. I should have known that you were worried about Me and searching for Me. I really am a child who must remain attached to you and permit you to make my decisions for Me. I am the cause of the tension you feel and I will be compliant so there will be no tension."

The other direction of Jesus' temptation at this point was to be defiant. He may have been angered by Mary's question and implication that He had plotted His action with the intent of upsetting her emotionally. He could have blown up in rage at her, blamed her for being irresponsible, or arrogantly suggested that she should have known he would be dealing with spiritual matters. By being compliant, Jesus would have treated Himself as less than He was created to be, and by being defiant He would have treated Joseph and Mary as less than they were created to be.

What Jesus did was to find a third alternative which was unexpected. This approach became characteristic of Him in His ministry, especially as people attempted to trap Him with questions to which they thought there were only two answers. Jesus was forever coming up with at least a third possibility which partially explains why His words have lasted. Perhaps finding a third alternative was something He learned at home. He certainly applied it in this exchange with Mary in the Temple. He walked the straight, narrow, thin line between compliance and defiance.

Jesus' question was addressed to Joseph and Mary, although Mary had done all the talking for her and Joseph. Jesus' question raises some questions. What were His Father's affairs? Was he referring to Joseph's carpenter shop of Nazareth? Obviously not, or Jesus would have asked that question in Nazareth. The place where Jesus asked the question indicates a gentle but definite move in taking the title of "Father" from Joseph and giving it to God. Israel predominantly regarded the father relationship as one of authority. Jesus was saying what Joseph and Mary believed but were not feeling at the time. God is the authority for life and Jesus was seeking to learn about the affairs of that authority. Joseph and Mary had encouraged Jesus, but they wondered why He chose now as the time and here as the place to become so interested in God's affairs.

Although Jesus' culture expected Him to grow up faster than our culture expects of its youth, He still had to wrestle with issues that any person faces when moving from childhood to adulthood. The primary issue that was focusing in Jesus' life at the time of His first visit to the Temple formed the question, "Who am I?" Jesus was developing the capability to reason more logically and to consider imaginatively what effect His actions would have upon His future well-being. He also began to evaluate His behavior in terms of ideals and ideologies. He was seeking reasons and meanings in life. His religious feelings were an important part of the search. His question, "Did you not know that I had to be involved in My father's affairs?" (Luke 2:49, author) also made a statement. He was involved in God's affairs as a means of keeping pathways into the future open in order to prevent premature conclusions before He had gained sufficient experience to judge properly what He wanted to do with His life.

Joseph and Mary did not understand what Jesus said to them. They didn't understand because His response was completely unexpected. Just after we had been seated in a restaurant recently, the waitress asked if we were ready to order. When we replied, "Yes," she walked away, then sheepishly retraced the five or six steps to take our order. She had so anticipated our answer that she heard what she wanted to hear, and it took her several seconds to understand what we said.

Jesus also was not understood by Joseph and Mary because He broke out of the well-established communication pattern of parent to child. He was responding to them as one thinking for Himself, while they were expecting Jesus to respond with frustration at worst, or great regret at best. When a different kind of response came, Joseph and Mary were unable to catch it all.

Jesus' parents also did not understand because they did not know what Jesus meant by "Father's affairs." To whom and/or to what was that a reference? Of course, much later it was easy for people to read meaning into Jesus' statement, a meaning which He may never have had in mind in making the statement. Jesus' statement was like a compass pointing in a direction rather than a roadmap marked with every stop along the way.

It seems evident that Jesus' first visit to the Temple in Jerusalem indicates He was moving toward an awareness of His relationship to God. No doubt the awareness had begun to surface through His participation in the synagogue in Nazareth. Regardless of how this awareness and understanding were heightened by His Temple visit, His status at home was not altered by it. He returned to Nazareth with His parents and lived the normal, expected life of a twelve-year-old boy who was becoming a man.

Mary remembered these events. She brought them out of her memory from time to time and reexamined them. When Luke asked her to tell her story, she already had rehearsed it many times in her own mind. Telling it to Luke was a pleasure because he sincerely was interested in what had happened to her.

This is the last reference to Joseph, which has given support to the theory that He died sometime between Jesus' first Temple visit and His baptism, often referred to as the eighteen silent years. Many questions arise from the silence. Did Joseph teach Jesus his carpenter's trade? Argument from custom would say that he did. How long did Joseph live? How many more Passovers did Joseph and Jesus attend together? After Joseph died, did Jesus take over the male responsibilities of the family? Was He both brother and father to His younger brothers and sisters?

Luke emphasized the humanness of Jesus in his summary statement about Him, indicating that He grew like everyone else mentally, physically, and relationally. He kept growing in all aspects of life. Luke's words sound very much like 1 Samuel 2:26. I suspect that Jesus kept asking questions, commenting, and discussing teachings He heard at the synagogue and the Temple. Jesus seemed to have a friendliness that won the responsive friendliness of people. Much later, in His most difficult days, only a few turned against Him. No antagonistic gulf separated Jesus from the masses. Actually, Mark said, "the common people heard him gladly" (Mark 12:37, KJV). He had a quality of friendliness and cheer that won loyalty and affection from others. These attributes began early in life in His home with Joseph and Mary. His relational skills continued to be enhanced by His worship of God and His relationships with the citizens of Nazareth.

Luke has given us a window through which to peer into the life of Jesus. He revealed Jesus to have been a curious, inquisitive person as a young boy. Apparently Jesus nurtured that characteristic throughout life. Jesus was a seeker, and the first words we have from Him are searching words. He was struggling to answer the question, "Who am I?" At least part of the answer was that He would be a question person rather than an answer person. The searching attitude of Jesus contributed to many of His statements becoming words that have lasted through the centuries.

Note

1. Barclay, *The Mind of Jesus* (New York: Harper and Brothers, 1960), p. 5.

2
The Committing Words of Jesus
Matthew 3:13-17

The early church spent bountiful energy retracing the life of Jesus. The resurrection was the stackpole around which the followers of Christ stuck together. As year after year passed it became more important to the early church to trace the life of Jesus from the resurrection backwards.

The events in Jesus' life which the early church highlighted were not nearly as important as the interpretations given to these events. Great events come just like any other events. They happen and only in retrospect do people discover that something of outstanding importance had occurred. Interpretations always are made on the aft side of events. When I think of a significant event in my life I can recall many of my feelings since the event but I have great difficulty identifying my feelings preceding the event. Getting on the other side of an event is even more difficult when one or more of the persons involved are unavailable to tell what happened and how they felt.

This is the situation with Jesus' baptism. Thirty years after the resurrection of Christ, several people considered it worthwhile to write about some of the events that occurred in Jesus' life. His baptism is one of those events. Reporting the baptism of Jesus indicates its importance. Obviously the event was important to Jesus and He probably described the event to His disciples. No doubt this underscored the value of the event for those who decided to compile written records of Jesus' life. It is reasonable to conclude that some of His family and friends witnessed His baptism and gave early followers their impressions and interpretations. In whatever manner the descriptions of this event were first formulated, the church has interpreted and reinterpreted the meaning of Jesus' baptism for twenty centuries.

Baptism by John the Baptist

In seeking understanding about Jesus' baptism, we need to begin by examining the significance of the baptism of John the Baptist. All four Gospel writers record baptism being practiced by John while only Matthew, Mark, and Luke record that John baptized Jesus. None of the Gospel writers give us any information about the preparation of John the Baptist for his prophetic ministry. They tell us nothing about his education, experience, or decision to preach and baptize. About all the facts we have are that his parents, Zechariah and Elizabeth, were old when he was born, that his mother and Jesus' mother were cousins, and that John was six months older than Jesus. Other information about John can be pieced together from knowledge and material that has been unearthed in archaeological digs and discovered from sources that describe events in Palestine during the first half of the first century AD.

Each of the four Gospel writers portrays John as thundering out of the wilderness, stopping at the banks of the Jordan River to baptize those who would repent. John the Baptist was a straight man. You may have met some straitlaced people in your life, but I doubt if any of them was as straight and narrow as John the Baptist. John wore camel's-hair clothes with a leather belt, drank no wine, ate bugs and wild honey, and stayed in the desert as a recluse. Maybe the desert diet and heat getting to him is what caused him to come roaring into town breathing fire and brimstone. John must have been a sight to see, to smell, and to hear! Often John has been portrayed as an anger-filled man bellowing his message in a fashion that both intrigued and frightened his audience. When his listeners overheated from their guilt stirred by his message, John cooled them off by baptizing them in the Jordan River. His contemporary religious leaders said John was demon possessed.

I suspect that we have read John's life and his preaching with too much venom. From too many pulpits the only tone for the call to repentance, change of direction in life, is anger. The tone of John's message was one of urgency but not necessarily one of anger or hatred. His voice was like that of Isaiah, a lonely one because it was the only one at the time calling for radical change. Doesn't the word of God strike the ears of people with the force of a hint? The roar of John's message was not so much in its volume and tone as it was in its urgency.

The story is told of a congregation that called a pastor. His sermons were described as brimming with "hellfire and damnation." He did not remain long as the pastor. It was learned that his successor also preached with strong "hellfire-and-damnation" tones, but the congregation seemed pleased with the second person as their pastor. A member of a neighboring church asked one of the deacons why the congregation seemed so pleased with the second person rather than the first. The deacon replied, "It is true that the sermons of both pastors were crisp around the edges with fire and brimstone. The difference is the first pastor preached like he hoped we would go to hell and the second preached like he hoped we wouldn't."

I suspect that whatever was the content of John's sermons, they were delivered with a tone of hope that listeners could and would change for the better. John's life-style, including his attire, his diet, and his spoken word, was part of his message. In Hebrew thought word and deed were inseparable. To speak was to act and to act was to speak. Thus Luke wrote that John preached a baptism of repentance.

Where did John get this idea of baptism? Had he been in the desert so long that his own body odor called for a bath? Did he conclude that the external cleansing he needed was symbolic of what everybody needed internally?

The Greek word, *baptizo,* means "to immerse." Josephus used the word to mean "to dye." The New Testament uses *baptizo* only in the literal sense "to dip in" (Luke 16:24; John 13:26) and "to dye" (Rev. 19:13). Baptize is used only in the cultic sense, infrequently of Jewish washings and otherwise in the technical sense "to baptize." This usage suggests that baptism was considered to be something new and strange.[1]

Baptism was well known in the pagan world as the door through which people entered many of the mystery religions. There are early examples of sacral water ceremonies in Babylon, Persia, and India. The Ganges and Euphrates Rivers came to have a significance to Eastern religions comparable with that of the Jordan to Judaism and Christianity. The common root for these customs is impossible to unearth. Whether or not John knew about sacral water ceremonies and baptisms in other religions is unknown. It is probable that some who heard him preach were familiar with these practices.

The process for a proselyte—one not born a Jew—to enter Judaism included baptism. There were three necessary elements involved for a non-Jew to enter Judaism: circumcision, baptism, and a sacrifice. The baptism was to be conducted in the presence of three witnesses. The candidates' nails and hair were cut and all of his clothing was removed. He was immersed in water so that his body was totally covered. When he was raised out of the water, the essence of the law was read to him, he was warned of dangers and persecutions, he confessed his sins to the fathers of his baptism. All of this was a means of acting out a total break with the past and was based on the many washings of the Jewish law for purification.[2]

By the first century AD Judaism was made up of three factions: Pharisees, Saduccees, and Essenes. The Essenes are not mentioned by name in the biblical material for a couple of reasons. The Essenes' theological position was that they should withdraw from the world. They had a passion for cleanliness and were convinced that the only way to live and achieve cleanliness was to withdraw totally from the world and the influences of anyone other than their own Essenes. Further documentation of this group's existence and life-style has been substantiated in accounts of the Qumran community recorded in the Dead Sea scrolls.

It has been suggested that the Essenes may have taken John the Baptist in when his parents died or that John became influenced by them fairly early in his life. Certainly it is possible that he associated with and was influenced by the Essenes. Evidence is clear that if John associated with the Essenes, he also broke from them because it was only for themselves that they were preparing the way of the Lord in the wilderness. John came out of the wilderness preaching a baptism of repentance. John may have been a straight and narrow man but he was neither as rigid nor as isolationistic as the Essenes were.

There does seem to be more than a coincidental connection between the demand of the Qumran community for holiness and the ethical demand of John. Both understood their demands to be internal ones and the close connection of the two demands is expressed in the Manual of Discipline of the Qumran community: "No one is to go into the water in order to attain the purity of holy men. For men cannot be purified except they repent their evil."[3]

Every generation has those who claim that promise and favor are based on pedigree. This was the situation which John challenged in his day. Often a challenge of the status quo is described as being loud and boisterous. John's approach, with his clothing and his baptism of repentance, was so different from what was familiar to the people that he has been portrayed as one yelling and screaming his message. I have known people who were confronted by a differing but mild-toned messenger who claimed they were being yelled at by the confrontational person. Confrontation often reverberates with amplification because of the challenge it is to the status quo whether of the individual or the society.

Already I have indicated that baptism was not new either to the Jews or to many Gentiles. There were some characteristics, however, about John's message that made his message and his baptism distinctive. The prophetic voice had been silent in Judaism for nearly three hundred years. John's manner, style, dress, and tone were akin to the Hebrew prophets, especially Elijah. Thus, John's approach attracted attention. Elijah's loyalty to God resulted in him opposing the worship of Baal fostered by Jezebel and Elijah's memory had been preserved through Elisha and a guild of prophets. Later generations remembered the mystery of Elijah's translation through a whirlwind (2 Kings 2:11) and anticipated his return as the forerunner of the Day of the Lord (Mal. 4:5). John's similarity to Elijah caused many to think he was Elijah, which John denied (John 1:21).

A further distinctive of John's preaching was his call to repentance. Periodically a voice summoned Israel to repentance and it was believed by many that if the nation would repent for one day, the Redeemer would arrive. To this point John had been preaching what had been preached before but with the renewed zeal, tone, and drama of a prophet. However, when John tied baptism to repentance and called for Jews to be baptized "to show that you have repented" (Matt. 3:11 a, GNB), he interjected a completely new and disturbing concept into the religious climate. From John's perspective, everybody—Jews included—desperately needed the cleansing that God alone could give. John confronted the Pharisees and Sadducees, warning them that family names and pedigree exempted no one from accountability to God.

John Baptized Jesus

John's manner and message struck a responsive chord in the lives of people and they flocked to the Jordan River to be baptized by him. One day Jesus was a part of the crowd that heard John preach and He stepped forward asking John to baptize Him. John refused. Why? Had he and Jesus met previously? That is probable at least, at some of the festivals in Jerusalem or some family gathering, but it is doubtful that they knew each other intimately. Jesus had been in Nazareth apparently learning a carpenter's trade, and John had been in the desert. Did John sense in Jesus a greatness that Jesus did not yet sense? Was John aware of some of Jesus' insights and inquisitiveness which began in the Temple but had been nurtured and cultivated throughout the intervening eighteen years? Was John so in awe of Jesus that He could not bring himself to baptize Him?

Many would argue that John recognized Jesus as the Messiah or that he already knew Jesus was the Messiah before Jesus requested baptism. A major problem with this foreknowledge position is that the Gospel of John indicates that John the Baptist learned that Jesus was the Messiah by baptizing Him (1:31-34).

It is evident that in his preaching John sounded a clear call for people to repent, for them to autograph their repentance by baptism, and John gladly baptized them. Exactly why John was stunned by Jesus' request for baptism is speculation because the Matthew, the only Gospel writer to record John's resistance did not tell us. Matthew did not interpret His resistance other than to identify John's feelings that he should be baptized by Jesus.

Jesus spoke a lasting word to John the Baptist when John resisted baptizing Jesus. What Jesus said sliced through John's resistance. Jesus' encouragement to John to baptize Him pointed toward cross bearing and cross living when He suggested that His baptism was "fitting for us to fulfil all righteousness" (Matt. 3:15). Through His questioning, contemplation, study at the synagogue, and His visits to the Temple, Jesus grew in His wisdom of God.

"Righteousness" as a Hebraic concept is foreign to Western minds. The term is used in the context of relationships and refers to the demands that relationships make. The covenant relationship of people to God is primary in the Old Testament. God would be their God if the Israelites would be His people. Faith is the fulfillment of the relationship to God because faith is putting one's trust and confidence in God which is the bedrock on which the covenant is built. God initiates or offers Himself in relationship to a person and the relationship is consummated when the person in faith promises himself or herself to God. The one who upholds the covenant relationship is identified as righteous. In this context God always is righteous because God consistently is faithful in keeping the promise to be our God. We fulfill righteousness or complete the relationship when we are faithful to God.

Apparently Jesus heard in John's message a clear and certain call for people to establish their relationship as the people of God. He acknowledged John's baptism as an appropriate sign of that covenant relationship. His statement, "it is fitting for us to fulfil all righteousness" may refer to Himself and John or to Himself and others who desired to be baptized by John.

Jesus' desire to fulfill righteousness was a lasting word because He was expressing a faith commitment to God that, by its very nature, was a choice against ultimate loyalty to anything or to anyone other than God. Later Jesus said it was impossible to serve two masters. To choose one was to choose against all others. To be faithful to God was to meet the demands of the relationship which fulfilled righteousness. Apparently John was convinced by Jesus' encouragement because he consented to baptize Jesus.

Problems with Jesus' Baptism

The baptism of Jesus by John is beyond question, but it is not beyond problems. This event is a problem in the Gospels although the authors make no effort to cover, excuse, or hide either the event or the problem which the event raises. John gives ample evidence in his Gospel of the ministry of John the Baptist, but only hints that Jesus may have been baptized by John (1:31-34).

Mark is the oldest Gospel and in it John's baptism is described as one of repentance. Mark also said that Jesus was baptized by John. Mark's Gospel has no record of John's resistance to Jesus' request to be baptized. The problem of Jesus being baptized by John whose baptism signified repentance was not a problem for Mark. Perhaps his writing helped surface the issue. Luke quickly, but briefly, recorded that Jesus was baptized.

Matthew most acutely felt the problem of Jesus being baptized by

John. His record of John refusing to baptize Jesus indicates the struggle which Matthew had. His struggle probably is indicative of the struggles which many of the followers of the Way were having with Jesus' baptism by AD 60.

The unanswered question is why was Jesus baptized by John. The problem has been intensified by the claim of the church that Jesus who was sinless asked to be baptized by John whose baptism was a sign of repentance from sin. Several answers have been offered through the centuries. Each of these suggestions has some truth and need not be antagonistic to the others.

Reasons for Jesus' Baptism

(1) Many say that Jesus was baptized to identify with human beings. This answer is helpful to some but raises at least two difficulties. This suggests that the baptism had no authentic significance to Jesus personally and begs the question of identification. No other event in the Gospels has Jesus going through the motions of an event. By being born a human being and growing emotionally, physically, and spiritually, Jesus had identified with human beings by being one. How did being baptized in the Jordan River enhance that identification?

(2) Some have suggested that Jesus was baptized to please His mother and family as is indicated in the Gospel according to the Hebrews. (This is an apocryphal book.) There are other examples of family pressures on Jesus and this one may have been among them. What personal authenticity did His baptism have if He were doing it either to please His family or to get them to cease pressuring him?

(3) Jesus had heard of the work of John the Baptist and the moral awakening that it was producing. He may have wanted to join His own comradeship and efforts with John.

(4) Perhaps the expectation of John's message aroused urgency in Jesus. The urgency was a signal that the search for direction and mission He had anticipated now was ready to begin.

(5) Jesus never thought of Himself in isolation. Thus He identified Himself completely with His nation's needs. Vicariously, he would be baptized into their need for repentance and with them and for them He expressed the urgency of commitment to the kingdom of God.

(6) Jesus' baptism is referred to by many as the fulfillment of prophecy (Isa. 11:2). Certainly in examining Jesus' life after His resurrection it was easy for His followers to say that the Spirit of the Lord

was upon Him. Nothing in Isaiah's prophecy suggests baptism as a sign of this. Jesus Himself clearly stated that it was what occurred internally rather than externally that demonstrated the presence of God.

(7) Since Jesus grew as a human being and faced life as a human being it seems appropriate that His awareness of Himself, who He was and who He hoped to be, were gradual developments that came through deepening awareness during His years in Nazareth. Is it not possible that in hearing the preaching of John the Baptist that Jesus heard the Word of God that struck a responsive chord in His life? Perhaps then He recognized that the opposite of repentance was to stay the course. He heard in John's word the clear call by which Israel could and must change the course. He sensed a new age was being ushered in for His people and for the world, and John was sounding forth the call to people in a way that it had not been sounded for generations.

Jesus saw the new age coming and sensed His desire and need to be part of that age. He stepped forth to be baptized, signaling a beginning. In that sense Jesus redefined the form—baptism—as He later pointed out that when forms, old wine-skins, had lost their usefulness and flexibility to carry the substance, new wine, the old wineskins should be thrown away and new wineskins should be used.

Interpreting Jesus' Baptism

Was not baptism an outward, visible sign of Jesus' commitment to ministry? The Synoptic Gospels have a similar sequence of events: the preaching of John the Baptist, the baptism of Jesus, Jesus' sojourn in the wilderness, the calling of disciples, and the expansion of ministry. The Synoptic writers intentionally portray the ministry of Jesus as beginning at His baptism.

Had not Jesus been questioning who He was? "Who am I?" is a question every human being asks in some form. In a sense an answer really cannot be given to this question. The best a person can do is to tell others the direction in which He is marching. This is what Jesus did in being baptized. He was baptized to signify the completion of His covenant with God saying to God and to Himself, "This is the direction I am going." His baptism was the time when the anchor was lifted, the cables were cut and Jesus' life set sail into the deep, charting a direct and difficult course. Is it possible that Jesus knew not every turn or every event, but it was a direction toward which He chose to move? Jesus may have been as surprised as anybody at some of the things that happened to Him along the way.

Not only did John's baptism of Jesus inaugurate Jesus' ministry but also revealed its unexpected nature. John presented his baptism as a washing from sin. Jesus interpreted baptism as repentance, and self-denial that led all the way to Golgotha. John invited people to be clean. Jesus called people to die. Jesus used the word *baptism* to refer to His own impending death (Mark 10:38).

Jesus' baptism also was a time of blessing, acceptance, approval, and assurance. Mark and Luke suggested that the communication of the blessing was between God and Jesus when they record "You are My beloved Son; in You I am well pleased" (Author's translation, Mark 1:11; Luke 3:21). In Matthew the voice announced "This is my beloved Son, with whom I am well pleased" (3:17) which seems to be his attempt to reconcile John's baptism of Jesus by suggesting that the blessing was for all who were present to hear. What the writers recorded is that God affirmed and approved of Jesus before He ever did anything.

Regardless of how you deal with the difficulty caused by Jesus being baptized by John, the church clearly has seen Jesus' baptism as His inauguration, commissioning, and ordination to ministry. In this regard Jesus' baptism was a beginning. It was not an ending nor was it an end in itself. Jesus' baptism was an outward expression of His inner commitment.

Certainly because Jesus was baptized is why baptism became important as the early church was forming. Various New Testament writers used a rich variety of meanings for baptism: forgiveness, rebirth, cleansing, death, resurrection, refreshment, adoption, light. For the early believers, baptism was patterned on the death and resurrection of Christ (Acts 2:38; Rom. 6:3-4; Gal. 3:27; 1 Cor. 12:13). In the biblical record of the early church, baptism means that the one being baptized is dying to the old life in sin and rising to a new life in Christ. Baptism signals a reshaping and redirecting of one's thinking because of the impact that the awareness of God's presence has had on the individual's life. Baptism is an act of commitment and promise in which the old life is buried and the believer is raised to a new life—new in direction, purpose, and objective. Baptism is an outward, visible sign of the inward, invisible grace of God at work in a person's life.

The words of Goethe are apropos: "The highest cannot be spoken; it can only be acted." Baptism serves as a seal of the promise of God's love, care, and presence. There is no recorded instance in the New Testament of the baptism of any persons other than new converts. Baptism has become a symbolic way of saying, "I am ready to grow. I willingly entrust myself to God's creative power to grow me beyond where I am." Thus baptism has become the signal of the dawning of a person's faith in God which completes the covenant relationship.

Baptism marks the dividing line between the old and the new. It is a signal that a person is beginning his faith commitment to God just as Jesus' baptism signaled the beginning of His faith commitment to ministry. A person does not know at the beginning of a journey all that is in store for him on the way. Did Jesus know every detail that would unfold during His ministry? Would He have anticipated that his disciples would have such a difficult time learning or that religious leaders would be so resistant to change.

A significant aspect of baptism is the interpretation given to it. The early church came to recognize that Jesus' baptism was the beginning point of His ministry. The early Christians looked back and recognized the significance of the event and gave it a place of importance in the gospel record.

From the biblical information available we can conclude that Jesus' baptism signaled His commitment of faith in His relationship with God which was a consummation of the covenant relationship. His baptism pointed in the direction in which Jesus was marching. He was setting sail on a course of life. It was a course that turned out to be very difficult and disturbing but a course on which He was willing to remain in spite of the many offers He was given to live differently.

Jesus' request to be baptized by John is a lasting word. It counters anything that anyone, including John the Baptist and Matthew, would expect the Son of God to say. It is such a difficult request that Matthew's Gospel has John refusing to baptize Jesus. Through the centuries this has been a difficult word of Jesus with which the church has had to deal. Some, like the author of John's Gospel, did not hear it as germane and found no need to mention it. Others, like Mark and Luke, saw Jesus' baptism event as important and reported it in a rather matter-of fact style. But there are those, like Matthew, who wrestled with the question of why was Jesus baptized. As Matthew told it, right in the middle of the Jordan River Jesus was challenged to change the course of His ministry before He ever began, but He refused. Jesus was interpreting the event of His baptism as a consummation of His faith in God which was essential to complete His covenant relationship with God or in His own words "to fulfil all righteousness."

Jesus' baptism signaled the direction He was moving. There were many times during the three years that followed when He was tempted to abort His mission. "Let it be so now; for thus it is fitting for us to fulfill all righteousness" have become lasting words. They are lasting words because Jesus remained faithful in His commitment to God.

Notes

1. Albrecht Oepke, "Baptizo," *Theological Dictionary of the New Testament,* Gerhard Kittel and Gerhard Friedrich, eds. (Grand Rapids: William B. Eerdmans Publishing Company, 1964) vol. 1, p. 530

2. William Barclay, *The Mind of Jesus* (New York: Harper and Brothers, 1960) p. 19.

3. Ibid, p. 22.

3
The Struggling Words of Jesus
Luke 4:1-13

Jesus' baptism was an external sign of His internal commitment to ministry. Having made a conscious decision about the direction of His life, Jesus went into the wilderness to explore and formulate both how He would minister and what His methods of ministry would be. I think it is no accident that in telling about the life of Jesus, Matthew, Mark, and Luke record successively His baptism and His wilderness temptations.

The wilderness temptations of Jesus surfaced the issues of security, power, and popularity. The way Jesus faced each of these issues instructs us about how we can negotiate the struggles raised for us by these same temptations.

Temptation

The English usage of the verb, *to tempt,* has a consistently negative meaning—to entice to do wrong, to seek to seduce a person into sin, or to attempt to persuade a person to take the wrong route. In teaching His disciples to pray, Jesus urged them to say, "Lead us not into temptation, But deliver us from evil" (Matt. 6:13). Perhaps no petition raises more questions than this one. Does God lead us into temptation? Does God test us to determine the strength of our moral fiber? Is God some type of Heavenly Psychologist who has designed the human experiment to measure how people respond to the options before them, and why?

If the only word we had about temptation were, "Lead us not into temptation," then many might conclude that God does the tempting. Some hold this view and substantiate it with the event in Abraham's life when he prepared to sacrifice Isaac. That event has been interpreted as a time of temptation and testing by God. If God does the tempting, then that at least makes Him an accessory to the crime. A person cannot be held totally responsible for the crime if God enticed him to sin.

The fall story of Adam and Eve, however, clearly locates the source of temptation with the serpent. The serpent is distinctly different and separate from God. Jesus, in the account of His temptation and testing struggles in the wilderness, reported that it was the evil one who sought to seduce Him into taking shortcuts. The evil one is separate and apart from God.

Diabolos means *obstructor,* that which opposes. It is an opposing force that has power. Many people support dualism, the forces of good and evil having equal strength, with the edge going to evil in this life and to good in the next life. Nowhere in the Old Testament is this the concept of evil. In the Book of Job, Satan acts more as an accuser or the prosecuting attorney. In 1 Chronicles, the common noun used for Satan denotes virtually a personification of human frailty. A person has a weakness that is personified and called Satan. Is this not what Jesus did later when He said to Peter, "Get behind me, Satan?" (Matt. 16:23).

That which obstructs a person from serving God and communicating His love may be identified as evil, the devil, or Satan. The principle weapon of Satan is fear and his primary methodology is the use of half truths. Collaboration with Satan results in misused or abused freedom that obstructs life, and therefore obstructs the presence of God. Scott Peck draws two conclusions about Satan that are helpful at this point: (1) Satan has no power except in a human body; (2) The only power that Satan has is through human belief in its lies.[1] These two conclusions highlight the difficulty in knowing where the person, especially the subconscious, leaves off and Satan begins. Thus *obstructor* is descriptive of Satan.

The Greek verb, *peirazein,* that is translated *to tempt,* has a different connotation. The basic force of this verb connotes testing with the intent to build up and make stronger. In this sense, temptation is an invitation and opportunity for growth. Eric Heiden, Olympic championship ice skater, illustrated this. His training exercises were much more demanding than any competitive skating event could ever be. Strength and stamina had to be developed and could only be done by putting himself "to the test" that was more strenuous than he would face in competitive skating.

It is correct that testing is a part of life. It is incorrect to say that testing is what God does to find out how strong or how weak we are. To hold that testing occurs to educate God flies in the face of fact that God already knows about us. Surely the One who knows the number of hairs on our heads also knows the pressure points of our emotional stability, as well as the struggles we experience with our commitment to Him. Some have altered this testing interpretation to suggest that testing occurs so we can know our strengths and weaknesses. However, even this interpretation makes God into a manipulator. God is seen as maneuvering events around in our lives to try to teach us our strengths and weaknesses while running the risk of destroying us during the experiment.

As Jesus told His disciples about His wilderness temptation experience, He said that being human involved searching out one's limitations. In this search a person may try to be more or less than she was created to be. To go either direction is to sin. Perhaps Jesus had this view in mind when He said that straight is the way and narrow is the gate that leads into the kingdom of God. It was Jesus' brother, James, who later gave a very clear and unprecedented statement about God not expressed elsewhere in the Bible.

> Blessed is the man who endures trial, for when he has stood the test he will receive the crown of life which God has promised to those who love him. Let no one say when he is tempted, "I am tempted by God"; for God cannot be tempted with evil and he himself tempts no one; but each person is tempted when he is lured and enticed by his own desire. Then desire when it has conceived gives birth to sin; and sin when it is full-grown brings forth death (Jas. 1:12-15).

We routinely fail to do the best of which we are capable. With each failure we wrong God, our neighbors, and ourselves. Constantly before us are invitations to yield to our desires, but these invitations are not extended by God. Evidently, Paul understood this to be true of life. He wrote to the Corinthian Christians (1 Cor. 10:13) that the difficulties they were experiencing were common. He added that God was the resource who enabled people to deal with hardship and who gave them strength not to sin.

Life is filled with temptations, and we cannot avoid them. To live life is to be confronted with choices. Temptations do not come from God in order for Him to know the stuff of which we are made. He already knows. Temptations afford us opportunities to grow or chances to regress depending upon our decisions. A temptation is a crisis. In the Chinese language two characters, one meaning *danger* and the other *opportunity,* are united to form the word *crisis.* A temptation is either a danger or an opportunity, depending upon how we respond to the temptation. We must evaluate where the path of each temptation seems to lead and determine which is the direction we need to move in order to be faithful and consistent in our commitment to God.

Wilderness Temptations of Jesus

Tradition has implied that Jesus experienced only three temptations, although Luke wrote that the evil one left Jesus for a season. Jesus was confronted with numerous temptations throughout His life. Insight into how Jesus dealt with temptations may best be examined by studying the Gospel accounts of His wilderness temptations.

Serious consideration of Jesus' wilderness temptations reveals that they were growth opportunities for Him. Jesus' wilderness endeavor was one of personal struggle. The Scriptural accounts of these temptations indicate that Jesus was alone. Therefore, He must have been the source for this information about His struggle which was a natural part of His human experience.

He was seeking direction to the question, "How do I bring people to God and God to the people?" This was the mission to which He committed Himself at His baptism. After making His commitment, He then sought routes to take in accomplishing the mission. Thus, He spent time in the wilderness.

Being alone for an extended period of time often results in plumbing the depths of one's life. The written accounts of the temptations describe Jesus' struggle as an inward one. There was no mountain in the wilderness from which all the kingdoms of the world could be viewed. In His mind, Jesus pictured the kingdoms of the world and contemplated how He might rule them. He seemed to want to rule them in the same manner He would rule in the lives of individuals.

During his contemplation Jesus was tempted by the devil or the evil one. The word translated *devil* means *adversary, obstructor,* or one who is the antithesis of God.[2] These shortcuts were evil because they required that Jesus compromise His worship of and commitment to God in order to use the shortcuts.

The Shortcut of Security

As Jesus wandered in the wilderness He wondered how He could persuade people to follow Him. A natural method came to mind—food. Why shouldn't He think of food? He had been fasting for a long period of time. His fasting stirred His hunger and the stones around Him reminded Him of bread. Could Jesus have thought, *Aha! This is one way to bring people to God: give them bread"?* An aspect of arrogance is contained in this temptation. The suggestion was for Jesus to give no thought to limits at all, to exercise His strength and use His power with no regard for any concern except Himself. Jesus was tempted to bypass the laws of reality that included planting, cultivating, reaping, grinding, and cooking. The arrogant temptation is to disregard the limitations of being human.

The first temptation contained double trouble offering a shortcut to security in bringing people to God. First, it was bribery. To offer bread to people in exchange for their willingness to come to God was to obtain followers for the sake of what they would get out of it. God calls people to a life of giving rather than getting. Many modern testimonies are filled with descriptions of material possessions, accomplishments, and successes. The implication is direct and clear that the testifier is propagating personal payoff for following God. The person is saying, "See what I got for following God." How many have we enticed to follow Christ for what they could get out of it? We fail to tell them that crucifixion is what authentic disciples may receive from discipleship.

The second mistake in the shortcut of security is that it deals with symptoms rather than the disease itself. Providing bread for the hungry is an emergency measure to keep them from starving; however, this is only a first step. To do nothing more is to make the hungry more dependent and indebted while the causes of hunger and other insecurities run rampant, ravaging the lives of millions across the globe.

In this first wilderness struggle about which Jesus told, He was tempted to be a cheap leader, to begin with security rather than to end with it; to bring outer abundance rather than inner holiness and wholeness. In telling the story of temptation, Jesus laid Himself bare, letting people see and feel His struggles and agony. Jesus concluded that the shortcut of security was destructive to His objective of bringing God to the people and the people to God.

An early event in my life was instructive to me later in understanding Jesus' resistance to shortcuts. Robert Percy was my fifth-grade Sunday School teacher, a fine man, the father of four beautiful daughters (I noticed later). I remember only one statement he made, "The longest way around is the shortest way home." The statement raised more questions for me than it provided answers, and so I filed it away under "Confusing Statements I Do Not Understand."

It was a year later that the confusion was cleared from this statement. I was invited to Ronnie Shearer's birthday party. Ronnie's parents took us to the picture show. After the movie, we began our walk to Ronnie's house for cake and ice cream. We were in view of his house when we came to a fork in the road. The long way was to the left, but the short route was to the right and went down by the creek. Being intelligent boys, knowing that three heads were better than one, we chose the shortcut by way of the creek. When we arrived at the creek, there were numerous things beckoning—rocks to be skipped across the water, puddles to wade, frogs to catch. Eventually we crossed the creek and headed up to Ronnie's house.

As we approached the house, I saw my parents in the front yard. First, I wondered what they were doing there. Then, in amazement I thought, *Surely it is not time for the party to be over.* Then I realized, *Howard, the party is over for you!* Was it ever! That day, the longest way around would have been the shortest way home for me.

Jesus was confronted by the option of turning stones into bread. Apparently He considered this possibility seriously and weighed the alternatives carefully. The temptation for Jesus was either to take a shortcut to meet an immediate need and gain security, or choose a different path, a longer route to meet the needs of people. The people wanted bread with or without the word of God. Jesus saw that He must give them the word of God, preferably with bread, but certainly the word of God at all costs.

The standards of Christ are not arbitrary ideals for exceptional people; they are the bedrock necessities of social life. We disobey at our peril. If we leave God, we can only go into the world without God and that world knows nothing of mercy or pity. That world entices us with a promised security that turns out to be a realized insecurity.

The shortcut of security was a real snare before Jesus. He could have stepped into that trap but He carefully weighed the consequences of that choice. Consider the strength that Jesus developed from this experience, and notice the lasting words in His statement, "Man shall not live by bread alone" (Luke 4:4). These words cut across the superficial solution that materialism supplies our every need and points to the cross living that involves the conscious giving of life for the benefit and edification of others.

There were other occasions when the shortcut of security reared its head to offer itself to Jesus: when the Pharisees asked for a sign of His sonship; when the high priest chided Him to save Himself; when the thief said, "Save yourself and us" (Luke 23:39). Surely Jesus' experience in the wilderness gave Him strength when He was tempted to take the shortcut of security. His living gives us encouragement to avoid the snare of the shortcut of security and illustrates that the longest way around is the shortest way home.

The Shortcut of Power

Matthew and Luke see the wilderness temptations a little differently. Matthew's order has the issue of power as the capstone drawing the other two together, while Luke emphasizes popularity as the climax. Following Luke's arrangement, how Jesus wrestled with the issue of power is examined next. Jesus knew He had power, as all people do. A question to be answered was, "How do I use my power to achieve my objective in life?" This was a question with which Jesus struggled.

Luke wrote that in a moment of time, all the kingdoms of the world flashed through Jesus' mind. Another question for Jesus was what kind of Messiah would He be? The adversary's view of the world was that it all belonged to him. The adversary made an offer he was sure Jesus could not refuse. All these kingdoms could belong to Jesus for the price of worship, of ultimate devotion to the obstructor. What is the one thing a person must give up if he is serious about serving the devil? He must give control of his life to the evil one. To seek status through power is the bottom line in serving the obstructor, while the bottom line in serving God is love, using the power one has for the benefit of others.

The word *power* is of Latin derivation meaning "to be able." Power is the ability to effect change and it is not of itself good or evil. The use you make of power determines its moral quality. The Old Testament has a consistent image of power that portrays God's creative and fulfilling energy. This energy is activated in the worshiper of God and through the worshiper to her societal situation.

Since Jesus perceived Himself as the anointed one, He wrestled with the question, "How will I use My power?" One temptation was to become the type of Messiah the world expected. Jewry envisioned the day when all nations would honor Israel. Six million Jews were scattered throughout the ancient world at this time. The Zealots were enraged with the oppression of Rome. The Pharisees were involved in religious activity and adhering strictly to the religious laws. The Sadducees were attempting to appease the Roman government and be actively involved in the Temple. Underlying these and other groups was this secret wish, "If only the right leader would come to make us a confederacy, then we could unite and be the people of God."

Danger probably appealed to Jesus. There was something adventuresome about the possibility of drawing this many people together. In addition to this appeal, Jesus had been commissioned as the right leader at His baptism. As Jesus envisioned the kingdoms of the world, He hungered for them. How He wished He might draw all of them together to follow Him. There was plausability in the feeling of Jesus that there was almost nothing He could not accomplish and that He had the power to do whatever He chose.

On the threshold of His ministry, Jesus was confronted with the end of His ministry and what means He would use to achieve that end. Many people have concluded that as long as the end toward which they are moving is basically good, they ought not concern themselves with how they get there. Invariably, this attitude deadens people's sensitivity to their ethical responsibility and they conclude that the best way to get along is to go along. Jim Jones used power this way in Guyana, where nine hundred people followed him in committing suicide. Perhaps it was observations of attitudes like this that prompted Karl Marx to conclude that "Religion . . . is the opium of the people."

This second temptation in Luke's account is a description of the power struggle that was alive in Jesus. It is the same type of power struggle that confronts us. This is illustrated for me in the actions of the two Adolphs of the Nazi party in Germany in World War II.[3] Apparently, Adolph Hitler had an incredible arrogance. He saw himself as a superhuman destined to rule the world like a god. He believed himself to be above all rules which applied to other people. He could break treaties, annihilate a whole race of people, and attempt by sheer power to impose his ruling hand over others. Adolph Hitler epitomized the arrogant side of the power struggle.

Adolph Eichmann was on the apathetic side. He was the official who was in charge of the final solution of the Jewish problem. Years later, when he was tracked down and put on trial for crimes against humanity, his only defense for his part in the atrocity was simply that *he was doing what he was told to do!* He defined himself as a cog in the machine—just one more bureaucrat who received from above and passed on below. He accepted no responsibility whatsoever for his part in the process. In these two Adolphs is a modern embodiment of the alternatives that Jesus faced in the loneliness of the desert.

Too often when people are in the midst of a crisis they are confronted with the necessity of a decision and feel bound by either/or alternatives. On many occasions, people, especially religious leaders, cornered Jesus with either/or alternatives. Invariably Jesus chose a third option as His solution to the issue. This is what He did with the question of how to use His power. The obstructor urged Him to choose either arrogance or apathy. Jesus chose to walk the corridor between arrogance and apathy by joining His power with the power of others for their benefit, not counting the cost to Himself. Not only in the wilderness, but also on other occasions, Jesus evaded the shortcut of misused or abusive power by walking the straight, narrow path between arrogance and apathy.

The Shortcut of Popularity

Jesus strolled through the wilderness feeling the sand under His feet and the sun burning on His brow. He reflected upon His baptism and gave serious consideration to His identity. Through His contemplation a question arose, "Am I really who I claim to be?" Within Himself was set the tension of a two-pronged question, "Who am I, and how do I communicate who I am to others?"

The highlight of His life had occurred only days earlier when He felt the presence of God in a keen way confirming, "Thou art my beloved Son; with thee I am well pleased" (Luke 3:22). "How ought the Son of God to live?" was another basic question for Jesus in this wilderness retreat. He began to think through some possible approaches He could use to communicate that He was the Son of God, and to consider what message He would bring to people. Jesus used His imagination. Isn't this one of the ways we work on a solution to an issue? We are confronted by an issue and we play out in our minds various alternatives to assist us in deciding on direction. So was the approach for Jesus.

He imagined Himself on the top of a wall of the Temple looking down into the Kidron Valley, 450 feet below. He envisioned many people gathered on the Temple grounds, as occurred during holy days. Jesus thought to Himself, *The people need to know who I am. Perhaps if I jump from this height, attention will be drawn to Me. I need to get people's attention in order for them to listen to Me.* Jesus understood that the Messiah was to come through the Temple, and this seemed an opportune way of coming through the Temple to the people.

As Jesus thought of His leap for attention, the adversary helped Him recall Psalm 91:11, "God will put his angels in charge of you to protect you wherever you go. They will hold you up with their hands to keep you from hurting your feet on the stones" (Luke 4:9, author). Note the half-truth that is expressed by extracting a verse out of context. How often we take this approach! When we want to travel in a specific direction in life but are struggling with the decision, we search for and find a passage of Scripture to support our desire.

At this juncture in Jesus' life He was tempted to twist the Word of God to fit His desire. Maybe if He did leap from this spot, God would take hold of Him and place Him safely in the valley below. People would see this sensational feat and be drawn to Him, He imagined. But Jesus thought further before He jumped. He concluded. "The sensational of today becomes the commonplace of tomorrow, and I would have to do ever-increasing sensational feats to keep people with Me." Jesus resisted the sensational approach of playing to the gallery.

There was another reason why Jesus refused to play to the gallery. His faith and commitment to God called for Jesus to take risks and assured Him that God would journey with Him. Nevertheless, Jesus saw the foolishness of putting Himself in a destructive situation just to see if God would protect Him from His own foolishness. Risk taking is to be done on the basis of confirmed faith, not as an intention to remove doubt so faith can be confirmed.

Jesus was tempted toward the sensational as a means to draw instant followers. Rather than rushing toward this temptation, Jesus stepped back from it, looked at it carefully, and saw here an opportunity for growth for Himself and those who would come after Him. He spoke a lasting word, "You shall not tempt the Lord your God" (v. 12). This word negated the understanding that God was at anyone's beck and call as a "Heavenly Bellhop" to do one's bidding. It was a lasting word because Jesus was choosing the long way of authentic care and love for others, what He could give to others rather than what He could get from them. This approach always is risky. It seldom is successful enough to satisfy the populace and, in their unrest, they turn on the one who is unsuccessful.

Jesus considered the shortcut of popularity, playing to the gallery. He thought of at least one way to receive instant, positive response; but He also saw the shallowness of this approach and the temporariness of such a response. He rejected the shortcut of popularity and chose instead the long route of service. Jesus was eager to minister to people and to draw them to God, but He resisted quick fixes and superficial methods to accomplish His task. He took the long way around and what He got out of it was a cross.

In the best sense of the phrase, "The way of the cross leads home." The way of the cross is that of service—giving yourself, spending your life for the express purpose of demonstrating and manifesting the love of God. When this is done, you can resist the shortcuts of security, power, and popularity. Jesus resisted the shortcuts in the wilderness and the adversary left Him until a more opportune time. Jesus was strengthened by His wilderness journey, but He was not immune to temptation. Other shortcuts were presented to Him throughout His ministry. I will examine some of those temptations in the next chapter and illustrate how Jesus refused to compromise the love of God. Jesus continually demonstrated that with temptation, the longest way around was the shortest way home.

The evil one wanted Jesus to give over control of His life; then all kingdoms would be His. In other words, the offer was to let someone else make decisions for Him. Then He would not have to agonize and struggle with difficult questions and issues. What the Gospels record is that Jesus' life was never lived free from struggle, agony, and temptation.

As an adolescent, when I heard or read about the temptations of Jesus, I concluded that He faced three temptations. When He had worked through those three, He was strong and able to face life, I thought. I longed for the time when I would have worked through my three temptations and would then be free of struggle and tension in my living. I missed a significant comment that Luke made, "And when the devil had ended every temptation, he departed from him until an opportune time" (v. 13).

Perhaps every temptation that Jesus faced and that we encounter is some variation of the temptation to security, power, or popularity. A closer, more serious examination of the Gospel accounts of Jesus' life reveals many opportune times arose when the obstructor offered Jesus a shortcut. Each time Jesus responded with a lasting word because He was committed to being the incarnation of the love of God. In every situation in which a shortcut was an option, Jesus chose the long way, because when love for God is the bottom line, the longest way around is the shortest way home.

Notes

1. M. Scott Peck, *People of the Lie: The Hope for Healing Human Evil,* (New York: Simon & Schuster 1983), p. 206.

2. Werner Foerster, "Diabolos," *Theological Dictionary of the New Testament,* Gerhard Kittel & Gerhard Friedrich, eds. (Grand Rapids: William G. Eerdmans Publishing Co., 1964) vol. 2, pp. 72-81.

3. John R. Claypool, "The Power Problem," sermon, Broadway Baptist Church, Fort Worth, TX, July 14, 1973, vol. 12, no. 24.

4

The Ministering Words of Jesus

Luke 4:14-30

The authors of the Synoptic Gospels indicated that Jesus' baptism signaled the beginning of His ministry. Following baptism Jesus was confronted by temptation in the wilderness. After the wilderness temptations, however, the Synoptists have different orders of events in Jesus' ministry. Matthew and Mark recorded the calling of four fishermen as disciples. Luke announced that Jesus' fame spread, and then He went to the synagogue in Nazareth where He read the Scriptures and taught. Jesus received mixed reviews for His public utterances in Nazareth. After reading the Scriptures, Jesus sat down and said, "Today this scripture has been fulfilled in your hearings" (Luke 4:21). The Scripture which He read was Isaiah 61:1-2, and 58:6.

The fulfillment of Scripture then, as now, was not a once-for-all event. The same Scripture may be fulfilled many times in many places. Luke recorded this event at the outset of Jesus' ministry. There were many times during His ministry when this Scripture was fulfilled. Was Jesus suggesting that then and there in the synagogue He was preaching good news to the poor, proclaiming release to the captives, giving sight to the blind, liberating the oppressed, and proclaiming the acceptable year of the Lord? Of course, this was neither the first nor last time that Jesus went to the synagogue because it was His custom to go to the synagogue on the sabbath. Surely, He spoke on other occasions when He was at the synagogue.

On first hearing Jesus the people were very positive. They liked Him and they marveled at His keen insight. What was as surprising as anything was that one of their own could demonstrate such promise. After all, they knew His parents, His brothers, and His sisters. They had watched Him grow up. It was difficult experiencing One that some of them had taught now saying some things that could teach them. There is an expression that states, "You can't go back home."

It has a dual reference. First, it suggests that once a child is grown and has been on his own, he cannot return to his parents' home and be a little child again. Neither he nor his parents can reverse the emotional process. Second, the statement refers to a person returning to his home community and being accepted as a mature, thinking adult. Of course there are exceptions to these generalizations, but the exceptions are rare.

The acclaim and adulation which Jesus received during this Nazareth synagogue visit were short-lived. Jesus began interpreting the Scripture He had read by giving illustrations from Israel's history. He chose two of Israel's well-known prophets, Elijah and Elisha, but He chose an event from each of their lives which His listeners had chosen to ignore. Both illustrations demonstrated the prophets relating to Gentiles in very positive ways. One of the quickest ways to be rejected is for a person to identify with the oppressed in the presence of the oppressors. This is what Jesus did with His illustrations. The synagogue congregation was so angry at Jesus that they ran Him out of town and were going to push Him over the bluff outside the city, but somehow He slipped away from them.

Luke packaged into Jesus' visit to the Nazareth synagogue a summary of the ministry of Jesus. The passage read from Isaiah outlines Jesus' ministry and the response of the congregation. First they praised Jesus. Then they sought to destroy Him.

Let us explore the outline of Jesus' ministry illustrating with recorded events how He sought to fulfill the Scripture on many occasions. Then let us examine some of the temptations which Jesus faced in His ministry and how His responses to these temptations solidified His opponents and fueled their desire to get rid of Jesus.

The Commissioning of Jesus

The opening words of the quotation from Isaiah have been used as a reference to Jesus' baptism. It was at His baptism that Jesus sensed a keen awareness of the presence of God and Jesus used His baptism to signal the direction He was living. Baptism represented His ordination or commissioning. It was an event which Jesus used to autograph His faith in and commitment to God and thus complete His covenant relationship with God. To be anointed by God carries the imagery of kingly coronation when oil was poured on the new king's head as the sign of blessing. To be anointed by God was a two-way communication in which God initiated the relationship and the individual was free to accept or reject the invitation. Jesus quoted Isaiah to illustrate both the mission to which God had called Him and His acceptance of the invitation with its attendant responsibilities.

There are at least four attendant responsibilities involved in the call to ministry which Jesus accepted: (1) to preach good news to the poor, (2) to proclaim release to the captives and to set at liberty those who are oppressed, (3) to offer sight to the blind, and (4) to proclaim the acceptable year of the Lord. There is no priority ranking of these responsibilities. They are of equal importance. What Jesus accepted as the tasks of His ministry He also taught as the responsibility of any who desire to be His disciples. Those who commit themselves to be His disciples commit themselves to the same tasks that He accepted. He said, "I am the light of the world" (John 8:12) and He said to his disciples "You are the light of the world" (Matt. 5:14). Thus, to examine the outline of Jesus' ministry is to examine the ministry of anyone who would be His disciple and would take the name Christian as an identity.

Good News to the Poor

In Hebrew thinking, word and deed are inseparable. To speak is to act. To talk is to do. To preach or proclaim is to announce, but it is announcing in the sense that the announcer is actively engaged in carrying out what he announces. Such comprehension is foreign to our minds in a culture where radio and television commentators make announcements with no investment in what they say. Should someone show some empathy for what he is saying then his empathy becomes worthy of comment, perhaps even derision.

Walter Cronkite announced the assassination of John F. Kennedy and another reporter reporting on Cronkite said that "Walter Cronkite obviously was shaken by the news," and the tone in the reporter's voice suggested that there was something unacceptable in Cronkite revealing his emotions.

For Jesus to preach meant for Him to act. There was never a need in Judaism to admonish someone to practice what he preached because putting into action was part of the preaching. One of Jesus' tasks was to preach good news to the poor. Good news is that which evokes joy in those who receive it, news that is undergirded by help and hope. Regardless of the situation, when good news is announced it means help and hope are available to those involved, no matter what the conditions. To be helpless and hopeless is to be devastated. On the human level when you are helpless and hopeless you are at best just existing. You may be breathing but you are not living. The word that is translated *good news* is used outside the New Testament as a technical term for victory. In its biblical usage good news contains this idea because the good news is that the circumstances have not overcome and destroyed you but that you have been able to journey through the situation and deal with the circumstances.

Jesus' task was to announce good news to the poor. The poor were those who were destitute of wealth and material, lacking even the necessities of life. The earliest biblical stories tell of the sensitivity that people were to have toward the poor. In the Old Testament the poor were the special charge of God and there are many warnings against the oppression of the poor. Paternalism is part of the oppression. Those who are poor don't want to be. Neither do they want us to buy them off with a food basket.

Mary Cosby told a relevant story.[1] She had been helping a woman, whom she had known for a long time, clean up her apartment in a low-rent housing development. Mary had noticed there was very little food in the apartment and it was the week of Thanksgiving. Mary went home, baked a turkey and took it to the woman on Wednesday before Thanksgiving. When the woman answered the door she did not reach out her hands to take the turkey. Mary said, "I've brought you a turkey for your Thanksgiving dinner." The woman replied, "Mary, why don't you help me get a job so I can buy my own turkey for my family?"

Recorded in Deuteronomy 15:1-11 are guidelines for people to care for the poor. People were to have open hands rather than hard hearts. Not one poor person was to be overlooked. This care for the poor was based on the understanding that the original lender was God and all had received bountifully from God. All decisions about possessions are decisions about God's property and the comments in Deuteronomy relate to attitude and action which are inseparable. The instruction given is that when a person sees a need, he is to open his hand. The opposite of an open hand is a closed hand which forms a fist.

There are numerous problems with this openhanded generosity that God encourages. There are con artists who take advantage of generosity. It is better to be conned than to refuse care to everyone because of the fear that someone will take advantage of your generosity. There also are those who would seek to become dependent on us and return again and again to receive from us. Not only must we be involved in emergency relief but also in long-term change. An Indian proverb states the need well: "Give a man a fish and he will have food for today. Teach a man to fish and he will have food every day." Part of our task as the light of the world involves working to alleviate hunger. Edmund Burke, the great British statesman once suggested that the only thing necessary for the triumph of evil is for good people to do nothing.

Deuteronomy 15:9 clearly indicates that stinginess is sin and that God's people are to be generous. Then there is the disturbing statement, "For the poor will never cease out of the land" (v. 11). This is the verse that Jesus quoted when Mary had used expensive ointment to anoint Him and people complained that the money could have been used more wisely.

What does it mean for the One who is to proclaim good news to the poor to say, "The poor will always be around"? Can you imagine what the reporters of the *Jerusalem Journal* did with that juicy quotation?

Dateline: Jerusalem. The disciples of Jesus are working overtime trying to clear the debris caused by the verbal bombshell that their teacher dropped on the city today. A source close to Jesus, who asked not to be named, tells of disarray and disillusionment among Jesus' disciples following His attempts to defend the waste of expensive perfume by an emotionally upset woman. Another unnamed source said it is nothing short of political suicide. Judas, the treasurer of the group, was reported to be on the verge of tears as he said, "It is as if He had said, 'If you've seen one starving peasant, you've seen them all.' "

This quotation, "The poor you always have with you" (John 12:8) that Jesus used was a disturbing word. It upsets our inactivity and shoulder shrugging and indicts us. First, it indicts us by saying that the very fact the poor are with us is evidence that we neither adopt nor practice God's economic policy of generosity and openhandedness. The problems of poverty and hunger are so huge we are overwhelmed, become immobilized, and seek a problem that is more our size.

Second, this word of Jesus indicts us because we have viewed ministry to the world in terms of competing priorities. People in the church tend to become Johnny and Susie one-notes for missions, evangelism, music, preaching, or social action. Does not this word of Jesus suggest that we are not to conclude that one thing is so important that all other things are to be left undone until it is finished? We have the opportunity to minister to the poor, to educate, to bring reconciliation, to serve God and one another. We need to keep the opportunities for ministry in perspective rather than in competition.

Jesus made His statement about the poor in the context of His defense of a woman who used expensive perfume to anoint His feet. In essence Jesus said of the woman, "She cannot love Me too much. She cannot give Me too much, because people who give themselves without reservation to God always have resources left over to give to the world." Jesus appreciated what the woman did which was in contrast both to the thoughtlessness of His disciples and to the superficial enthusiasm of the crowds. Jesus was not suggesting that the care of the poor was unimportant or casual. The good news that Jesus proclaimed was that God was always on the side of the poor, working with them to free them from the constraints of poverty. We are on God's side to the extent that we are found on the side of the poor, working for their victory and liberation from bondage.

Release the Captives, Liberate the Oppressed

When Jesus preached good news to the poor, He was releasing the captives and liberating the oppressed. Of course, poverty is not the only captor or oppressor. Fear, prejudice, possessions, disease, and religion oppress people and hold them captive. Jesus was the great Liberator. His words and deeds were offered to free people from anything that enslaved them and kept them from being persons created in the image of God. Perhaps the most comprehensive yet succinct liberating statement Jesus made was the Beatitude section of the Sermon on the Mount.

This sermon of sermons has been heard in a variety of ways. Some sentimentalists boast that the only religion they want is the Sermon on the Mount. I wonder if they have read it. Some who are troubled by its heavy demands give up in despair, concluding that it is unrealistic and impossible. A few have attempted to follow it literally, even to include self-mutilation. Others understand it as an interim ethic, intended for a brief period just before an expected end of the world.

There are those who suggest that the Sermon applies to the clergy only while others suggest it refers to relationships within the church but not in the world. Jesus did not endorse such double standards. Rather, He suggested that people develop the Beatitude attitude in their living in order to be free at last.

When Jesus began His now-famous sermon, people knew what He was going to say, "Repent, judgment is coming. God is angry." Even when these negatives are true, they are seldom helpful. Jesus surprised the crowd with His statement, "Blessed are you," when "Woe to you" was expected. His hand was not a clenched, smashing, repulsing fist, but an open hand, a gesture of giving, accepting, and receiving. No one is healed by judgment and punishment; the negative tends to make people sick. The Beatitudes portray the open hands of God reaching out to care for people in the midst of oppression and captivity.

Spiritual Bankruptcy

The Beatitudes as Matthew 5:1-11 recorded them deal with the question of liberty for the oppressed. They identify the steps by which a person moves from enslavement as a citizen of the world to become a liberated citizen of the kingdom of God. According to Jesus the first step is to be poverty-stricken. What did Jesus mean, "Blessed are the poor in spirit"? The poor in spirit are those who recognize their needy condition and seek the One who can supply their needs. The poor in spirit are neither the poor spirited nor the proud spirited. The poor spirited are devoid of spark and responsiveness. The proud spirited are stuck on themselves. Those who are stuck *on* themselves are stuck *with* themselves. The poor in spirit are blessed, not because of the condition, but because of where the condition leads. The poor in spirit are those who recognize and admit that by their own power they are utterly bankrupt to meet life. Then they begin searching beyond themselves for help and strength discovering that God is the Source of all that they need.

Jesus attracted all types of undesirables to Himself. Like a magnet He drew sinners and sufferers from their hiding places. Much of that magnetic power was expressed through the Beatitudes and reversed human values. Jesus stood the test of misery and the miserable flocked to Him. No one was off limits to Jesus and He did not close His eyes to anyone's suffering.

One of the things that cancer patients are teaching us is that people in the process of dying want others to open their eyes to their suffering and their ears to their conversations about death. Cancer patients want to be accepted so they can share their feelings. They are grateful to anyone who will enter the slum of suffering where they live.

The cancer patient epitomizes all of us. Totally on our own we are utterly helpless, and it is in recognizing our helplessness that we discover God helps those who know they cannot help themselves. The process that results in spiritual bankruptcy is similar to what happened to Jim. After my grandfather's death, Jim purchased my grandfather's business. I can see the excitement in Jim's face as he preened around the store after the sale had been finalized. He was enthusiastic and energetic. He had every intention of making the business more successful than ever because now it was his. As the months passed, Jim's countenance expressed more burden than joy, more trouble than excitement. Jim avoided conversations. He became less and less visible. It was rumored that he owed creditors large sums of money. He became nonchalant about the business and refused to pay his bills.

Then the announcement came. Jim had filed for bankruptcy. What a painful decision! What a blow to Jim's self-esteem! Of course the town's wagging tongues were not helpful. Everyone who knew little about the business had advice about how bankruptcy could have been avoided. Jim had failed in business and his body language communicated that he felt like a failure as a human being. Jim lived in seclusion for several months, venturing out into public only when it was absolutely necessary. Jim's plummet eventually bottomed out and he discovered that life had more to offer than business success or failure.

The process by which the poor in spirit hear the good news is similar to Jim's business experience. He tried everything he knew to do, resisted giving in, but eventually Jim had to declare bankruptcy in order to have any chance at living. You and I try everything we can think of to avoid hitting bottom spiritually. We attend church more often, participate in additional church-related functions, read the Bible, pray. There must be some religious hoop to jump through to solve the dilemma! These approaches may supply some temporary hope but until we declare spiritual bankruptcy, acknowledging that only God can help us, we will remain captives of our own efforts. The audit sheets of our lives reveal that we are in hock so far that we can never get our lives balanced and out of debt. Only if we declare spiritual bankruptcy will we permit the resources of God's love to balance our lives and ground us in permanent hope.

Mourning and Meekness

Do the words of Jesus ever seem totally irrelevant to you? Consider the next two Beatitudes in Jesus' famous sermon. He calls for mourning and meekness. The world says, "Enjoy" and Jesus says, "Grieve." What a contrast! Will anyone find liberation in the suggestion that happiness is tied up in grief work?

What could Jesus possibly mean by saying, "Blessed are they that mourn: for they shall be comforted?" (v. 4, KJV). Certainly He learned that grief was not happiness. He wept at the death of Lazarus and grieved deeply for the city of Jerusalem. Grief disfigures and slays. I am made aware often how grief distorts a person's voice. I have difficulty recognizing a familiar voice on the telephone when the person is overcome with grief. No one is exempt from the emotionally debilitating experience of grief which is the natural reaction to a significant loss.

How are we to understand this mournful attitude? Here are four interpretations. First, this Beatitude can be understood as a reference to persons whose lives have been invaded by death and are grieving over their loss. Understood this way, Jesus is saying, "Blessed are they that accept their own sorrow with the resolve to learn from their pain because they will experience comfort." It is possible for grief and mourning to stimulate people to plumb depths of life they never would examine were it not for their painful sorrow. This process may bring release to those held captive by fear of death or insecurity of dealing with life's crucial issues. Of course it is possible for those who are grief-stricken to become frozen emotionally and have all of life colored by bitterness and resentment. Surely Jesus is not saying that the morose, the miserable, or the sullen are the blessed or happy ones in life.

When loss occurs a person is driven to the depths of life and through such shattering she may experience a new strength and beauty. No one needs to seek a mournful, grief-causing experience hoping to gain strength and beauty. No one is long in this world before such events occur and when they do, learning and growth may result. There are stars that can be seen only in darkness and there is strength and vitality that may only be revealed through grieving. Jesus came to proclaim liberty to those held captive by grief.

A second understanding of the mournful Beatitude is to identify the mourners as those who voluntarily share the pain of others. These are the people who are desperately sorry for the sorrow and suffering that is being experienced by a fellow human being. Those who voluntarily share the pain of others could have avoided it easily enough with the assessment, "It's not my business; I have enough troubles of my own."

The mourners are those who expose themselves to the world's misery. They lend their strength, as feeble as it may seem, to the home where death has invaded. They are found at the jails, believing in those whom society has labeled hopeless. The mourners agonize over the slum dwellers, seeking to lighten the load of those whom life seems intent on snuffing out. The compassionate people in life are the mourners who empathize with others, placing their lives alongside those who are down and nearly out. Jesus called blessed those who voluntarily share others' pain because not only have they been released from oppression, but also they are at work releasing others.

"Blessed are they that mourn" may be understood in a third way— those who mourn because they have sinned. People usually are more concerned with evils that befall them than with sins they have committed. Much of life is lived unexamined. Time is not taken and energy is not invested by many persons to see if there be any sin in them, but the mourners see God as grieving over their sins, and they grieve, too. The mourners have declared spiritual bankruptcy which has quickened their consciences. With the sensitiveness of the psalmist, the mourner says, "Have mercy on me, . . . O God, my sin is ever before me. Against thee, thee only, have I sinned" (Ps. 51:1,3-4). Those who mourn for their sins will become better rather than bitter and thus be released from the captivity of bitterness and resentment.

A fourth interpretation of this Beatitude has an even deeper application. Blessed are they that mourn for their neighbors' sins. There are few such mourners in any age. Few people are troubled by the shame of the streets, the greed of the marketplace, and the violence of nations unless they fear they might be injured or their property value might decline. Numerous people will pass judgment on those who sin but few people will mourn for and with their neighbors because of their neighbors' sins and count themselves guilty in the common guilt of sin.

Whether people mourn as a natural response to personal loss, because of sharing another's pain, because of sin, or because of another's sin, Jesus said that comfort is the result of mourning. To be comforted does not mean to become comfortable. Comfort means, "To call to the side of." To mourn because of sin is to summon the aid of God because God alone can take away the guilt of sin. This comfort often is conducted through human voices and human embraces of love, acceptance, and forgiveness. These conductors of comfort are those who have mourned and been comforted.

The French have a saying that is apropos, "To suffer passes away; but to have suffered never passes." Those who have suffered come to the side of those who are in grief. Family stress and conflict are reduced not by making homes more comfortable but by making them more comforting. The person who cares intensely for the suffering and sorrow of others is blessed, because after knowing personal poverty, you can be sensitive to the suffering of others. Jesus' words, "Blessed are they that mourn" seems to cut across all logic; yet, are lasting words that release those oppressed by loss, by sin, and by guilt. Happy are those who mourn because God will come to their sides with tenderness and reinforcement. They will be comforted and they will become conductors of comfort.

As Jesus sought to proclaim liberty to the captives and release to the oppressed He suggested that mourning and comfort were the seedbed out of which meekness grows. Perhaps no word confuses our comprehension or our efforts more than this word *meekness.* It has been equated with weakness but meekness and weakness are antonyms rather than synonyms. The meek are not timid souls living in mortal fear nor are they doormats of life on whom all who wish may wipe their feet. Only two biblical characters are described as meek, but what a pair—Moses and Jesus! Moses defied the might of Egypt. Jesus could not be cowed by a powerful Roman official. Neither Moses nor Jesus was harmless or spiritless.

Meekness is the opposite of aggression. Aggression is a tightfisted, brute force-taking approach to life. Meekness is an openhanded, gentle, receiving approach toward life. Whatever is taken by force must be maintained by force. Watch two small children. One grabs a toy from the other. Having grabbed the toy, the grabber must now clutch it, hover over it to keep it because the grabee is looking for a chance to use force to grab it back. Watch two nations. The same principle is operative in international relations, but the stakes are higher and the potential for destruction is greater. Meekness is an openhanded sharing. Few people and fewer nations demonstrate any interest in being meek.

Meekness is power blended with gentleness. Meekness and humility are synonymous terms meaning teachableness. The meek are people who can and will learn because the first step to learning is the realization and admission of ignorance.

The Greek word *praos* is translated *meek* in the New Testament. It is the same word used to describe the taming of wild animals and describes strength and energy that has been harnessed or channeled for constructive use. Hyperactive children have the ability, energy, and desire to learn; however, they are easily distracted because they are sensitive to many stimuli and unable to filter out some stimuli. They become disruptive to others and frustrated with themselves. The challenge for parents and teachers of hyperactive children is to aid them in harnessing their energy and sensitivity in a direction toward a goal. The meek are those who seek to focus their instincts, impulses, passions, their mental, emotional, and physical energies in a constructive direction.

Many conclude that the path of meekness is too long and difficult. People look for a shorter route convinced that the course of least resistance is quicker and better. The path of meekness is difficult but strengthening. Out of mourning comes comfort and the comfort strengthens people making them pliable for learning. The French translation of the meekness Beatitude reads, "Blessed are the debonair." That sounds superficial and flashy but the underpinning logic is that the meek person is one whose strength is disciplined in such gentleness that he carries his virtues with easy grace, tossing off insults, and refusing to be burdened by carrying grudges. There is much that can captivate and oppress people including sin, guilt, resentment, bitterness, and force. Developing meekness, seeking to be teachable is the way out of captivity.

Desiring Righteousness

None of Jesus' ministering words were spoken in a vacuum, nor do they apply in a vacuum. The Beatitudes are illustrative of this in how each builds on the previous one and serves as the connective tissue for the one following. This understanding is evident with "Blessed are

those who hunger and thirst for righteousness, for they shall be satisfied" (v. 6). The awareness and confession of spiritual bankruptcy
leads one into mourning. The comfort of God enables the mourner to
be teachable and one who is teachable discovers a thirst for righteousness.

Jesus urged His disciples to have desire, the desire for righteousness. Because of our nature as human beings, once we set our minds
or wills in a direction, it is nearly impossible to move us off course.
Our difficulty often is a refusal to commit ourselves in a direction. We
may give lip service, but anyone looking into our eyes can tell the
desire isn't there. Once a rather pious churchman was reproving his
neighbor for using profanity. The profane neighbor replied, "Well, I
cuss a lot and you pray a lot, but neither of us really means what he
says."

Jesus spoke a disturbing word when He said satisfaction, fulfillment
would come to those who hunger and thirst after righteousness. This
is a troubling word because it suggests that we lay aside everything
else in order to pursue righteousness. As mentioned in chapter 2,
righteousness is completing the covenant relationship with God by
putting one's faith in God so that the relationship is sealed. God's
intentions and purposes in life become mine.

Jesus said righteousness comes to those who hunger and thirst for
it. This hunger and thirst are recurring longings. Hunger and thirst
are difficult concepts for many of us to comprehend. The closest we
get to hunger is when our gastric juices shift a little and we eat a
between-meal snack. About as thirsty as we ever get is from pushing
the lawn mower for thirty minutes in the summer heat. We stop, go
in an air-conditioned house, put ice in a glass, and turn a faucet. There
is water and our two-minute thirst is quenched.

The craving for righteousness that Jesus identified as a Beatitude
attitude is a physical hunger and thirst known by people whose desire
for food and water is so great that death is imminent if they don't
receive them. Hunger and thirst are signals of health and of needs. The
survival instinct has caused people to be cunning hunters, rugged
farmers, and educated agriculturalists. Out of a craving to survive
people have sought food and water. Jesus said it was this kind of
craving for righteousness that would be satisfied. He was depicting a
longing that means the difference between life and death. The require-
ment that Jesus laid out for His followers is not righteousness; rather,

it is the hunger and thirst after righteousness whose by-product is happiness, satisfaction. We are to crave righteousness with the intensity that a starving person desires food. Such craving calls for a commitment few are willing to make.

This invitation to crave righteousness frees us from the captivity of both fatalism and accidentalism so that our lives can be lived intentionally related to God. Life is composed of at least three groups of people: those who let things happen, those who don't know what is happening, and those who make things happen. It is fairly easy to become enslaved to fatalism which tells us that the course of events in our lives has been programmed and all we can do is wait for the events to happen to us. Such a view turns people into microchips who are at the mercy of a universal computer. There is no freedom, no blessedness, and no life in this approach. The ministering words of Jesus seek to cut across such thinking and living, and set us free to chart our courses toward righteousness because that is our desire and intention. Jesus seeks to free us from the captivity of fatalism so we may hunger and thirst after righteousness which will bring fulfillment.

At the other end of the spectrum of happenings is accidentalism. Proponents of accidentalism claim there is no order to life. Events transpire at random and any correlation between anything that people do and the events that impact on their lives is purely coincidental according to the accidentalists. About the only law that accidentalism accepts as valid is Murphy's law which states if anything can go wrong, it will. Jesus seeks to free us from accidentalism so that our lives can have some order. As we discover order, we may discover purpose. When our lives have purpose we begin to hunger and thirst after righteousness.

Mercy Givers

Liberation from fatalism and accidentalism leads to the pursuit of righteousness that includes being merciful, pure in heart, and a maker of peace. This kind of intentional living is not without risk, including the strong possibility of persecution. The intentional desire for righteousness involves being merciful to others which results in receiving mercy. Mercy is the ability to get inside another's skin until I can see things with his eyes, think things with his mind, and feel things with his feelings. An American Indian proverb says it well, "Don't judge a man until you have walked two days in his moccasins." Hosea, the

Samaritan of Jesus' parable, and Jesus Himself are biblical examples of mercy. Mercy is demonstrated by the person who goes the second mile, as Jesus urged, because of His compassion, not because there is a special reward for second-milers.

We can gain a better understanding of mercy by examining forgiveness because their natures are synonymous. Forgiveness is a rare commodity in our society. People bury the hatchet but carefully tuck away the map where the hidden hatchet lies. Forgiveness is essential for relationships to be maintained because hurt and estrangement occur that can only be dealt with by forgiveness. Forgiveness is a change of attitude within the one wronged. It means to forego all private revenge and to give up the right to retaliate. When you have been wronged, you have every justification to get even. The law is on your side. Friends support you. Often, even your enemies will admit you have a point. Forgiveness involves acknowledgement that one has been hurt and estranged and to become aware that the one who caused the estrangement has been hurt by causing the estrangement. Forgiveness is an unashamed admission that the relationship is more important than holding a grudge, revenge, or retaliation.

There are some misconceptions about forgiveness. "Forgive and forget" is unsolicited advice offered by bystanders but this is impossible unless a person experiences selective amnesia. How will the offended person become aware of any contribution she made to the estrangement if she forgets the entire situation? To forgive neither cancels nor undoes the damage or the offense; rather, the offended person forgoes the attempt to get even and seeks to continue the relationship. Forgiveness and forgetfulness are not synonymous.

A second misconception is that forgiveness means to pass over a broken relationship and say, "It really doesn't matter." Relationships do matter and it is the admission of their importance that will cause one to seek to forgive another, rather than to gloss over the breach.

A third misconception of forgiveness is expressed as condescension and goes like this, "You have hurt me deeply, but I will bear it." This is merely a form of one-upsmanship that continually reminds the offender of his offense. It keeps the estranged feelings buried alive by establishing a superior-to-inferior relationship. The offended one uses his position of having been offended to wield power over the one who caused the estrangement. Forgiveness is not authentic when the offended person maintains a superior position by claiming to forgive, saying the offense doesn't matter, or saying he will bear the hurt.

We are captives of condemnation, blaming others as well as ourselves. There is a way out of this hell and it is wrapped in the nature of mercy and forgiveness. It is the nature of mercy and forgiveness that receiving mercy is related directly to giving forgiveness. Those who demonstrate mercy also receive mercy. You do not earn forgiveness; that would be mercy by reward. The condition of the unmerciful person is such that she is incapable of receiving mercy. One who is incapable of giving forgiveness is incapable of receiving mercy because she is blind both to what mercy is and to her need for it. What blocks the flow of mercy from a person also blocks its flow to her. A law of physics states that for every action, there is a reaction. If there is no action, then there is no reaction. Without the action of giving mercy there is no reaction of receiving mercy.

While walking around the farm with my grandfather we stopped near an electric fence. I touched a blade of grass to the wire but felt no electrical shock. Immediately I told my grandfather that there was no current flowing through the electrical fence. He took hold of the fence and received an electrical shock. I touched it and received no shock. Then he looked down and noticed I was wearing rubber overshoes. I could not experience (feel) the current because my overshoes kept it from flowing through me. This is how it is with mercy. We cannot experience mercy for ourselves unless mercy flows through us to others.

The willingness to forgive is limitless. Mercy begins as an attitude and ends in an action. Peter asked Jesus if seven times were not the limit of forgiveness. Jesus responded that one ought to forgive either seventy times seven or seventy-seven times (the exact translation is unclear). Whether to forgive 77 times or 490 times is not the point because to keep count reveals one's interest in retaliation rather than forgiveness. Instead of endless revenge, the disciple of Christ is to practice endless forgiveness.

The way of the world calls for retaliation, an eye for an eye and a tooth for a tooth. Retaliation produces revenge and we become captives of condemnation. Jesus spoke a word that cut across the way of the world. He said the way out of condemnation is paved with forgiveness and mercy. To forgive another is to lay down one's life for the benefit of the relationship with him. Jesus spoke a lasting word that calls for a cross action which will put one crossways with the world. It is a word, an action, a way that liberates people from condemnation.

Pure Hearts

"Blessed are the merciful" is an appealing Beatitude. "Blessed are the pure in heart" is a difficult one but it is not by accident that purity follows mercy. The person who forgives is able to receive forgiveness that leads to the singleness of vision of which Jesus spoke that results in gaining glimpses of what God is like.

When the term *heart* is used in the Bible, it is a reference to the center of personality rather than to the muscle that pumps blood. The word *pure* seems to have a double-edged meaning—rightness of mind and singleness of motive.

No doubt when Jesus used the phrase "pure in heart" He was contrasting the internal cleansing of a person's life to the external cleansing of the hands or body. Jesus was describing integrity as opposed to duplicity. Integrity is wholeness. The integration of life means I reveal who I am. Thus purity of heart and wholeness are linked together. The outward life reflects the inner purity. This is in opposition to the hypocrites who have duplicity. They have two gods, one for the inner life and another for the outer life. People are hypocritical to the degree that they are incongruent. When people appear to have a rightness of mind and singleness of motive outwardly but inwardly are fueled by many motives, they are not pure in heart and are cursed rather than blessed.

Conflicting loyalties cause people to keep their eyes on two masters. That makes them cross-eyed and their vision is blurred. The eyes of the inwardly and outwardly pure are single, focused on one objective. Jesus said that if a person's eye is single, in focus, his whole body will be full of light. The pure in heart see God in the world around them when others are blind. The pure in heart are aware of the presence and movements of God in their lives even, perhaps especially, in the midst of pain. Those with a clear rightness of mind and singleness of motive in their personalities are the ones who are able to see God.

Makers of Peace

Undergirding the Sermon on the Mount is Jesus' encouragement that His followers nurture and develop the Beatitude attitude. Each Beatitude is intricately related and integrated with all of the Beatitudes. At the center of the Beatitude attitude are forgiveness, purity, and peace. Forgiveness means to forego all private revenge, to remit the right to retaliate. Forgiveness is essential if we hope to see God because only by forgiving others are we able to recognize and accept forgiveness for ourselves. Forgiving and being forgiven purifies our lives. Then are we prepared to take initiatives toward making peace. The makers of peace are the ones who are called to be the sons and daughters of God.

Practically everyone clamors for peace but the world has multiple shades of meaning and usage. A father shouts, "Give me a little peace and quiet." A troubled wife begs for peace of mind. Citizens of war-torn Ireland, Afghanistan, and Nicaragua want an end to fighting. The compulsive person wants peace from driving her life so she can live life. What do you want when you plead for peace?

Shalom and *eirēnē* are the two biblical words translated *peace.* The former is Hebrew and the latter is Greek; the basic meaning of both words is the same. Everything that works for the highest good of a person is the biblical understanding of peace. Peace is an inclusive term that holds all the positive aspirations of human beings, including wholeness, fulfillment, well-being, and joy. There really is very little debate about the desire for peace; yet I question how authentic the desire is for peace when so many actions perpetuate stress, strife, conflict, and war. Certainly part of the difficulty is that we seek the wrong means to arrive at peace. Thus we become slaves to our methods. We need the liberating word of Jesus to set us free from oppression, much of which is of our own making.

Harry Emerson Fosdick told the story of a man in New York City who decided to go to Detroit. He went to the bus station, bought a ticket, boarded the bus, and rode all night and well into the next afternoon. Upon arriving at his destination the man was profoundly shocked. He was in Kansas City rather than Detroit. What had happened? He had gotten on the wrong bus. There was nothing wrong with his intentions in New York City, but his good intentions had to be coupled with getting on the right bus in order to arrive at his desired destination.

Our intentions for peace are good but we take the wrong bus and find ourselves in shock when we do not arrive at peace. We claim we want peace but the buses of selfishness, force, and retaliation will not take us to peace. Currently many people espouse the attitude of looking out for themselves as the bus to peace. The argument goes that if you don't look out for yourself, no one else will. Basically, this philosophy concentrates on what *I* want, when *I* want it, as *I* want it. Consideration of the needs of others is secondary, at most. The concept of interdependence is nearly nonexistent. Wherever there is a lack of peace on the earth, chances are great that blind self-concern is not far behind. Selfishness holds us captive and regardless of how hard and fast we drive it, the me-first bus will not arrive at peace.

Force or violence is a second wrong bus. The idea has been around for centuries that peace can be brought about by force or violence. Jesus grew up and lived under the Roman occupation of Israel. He and every other Jew longed for the day when the occupation troops would pull out. Some of Jesus' statements ignited that hope and people encouraged Him to use force to defeat the Romans. Jesus resisted using violence and, when Judas saw Jesus backing away from forceful overthrow, he attempted to manipulate Jesus into a use of violence. Jesus resisted even then and the result was His crucifixion. Jesus was perceptive enough to see that even violence done to Him was not reason for Him to respond with violence. That was not the bus that would bring peace.

On every level of life force and violence are attempted as ways to peace. Many parents believe that verbal violence, belittling and demeaning children with words, will produce well-motivated and integrated personalities in their children. Children respond in kind with kind. They use the approaches to solve problems which are demonstrated to them and with them in their relationships. Karl Menninger, noted psychiatrist, aptly has stated that we learn to resolve hostility in our homes or we don't learn it at all.

How we deal with conflict and hostility at home becomes the pattern we use at school, at work, and with our neighbors. Solutions to conflict or the lack thereof, on the national and international scene reflects a culmination of individuals' approaches. Out of fear and insecurity, nations seek peace by building bigger and more destructive weapons of violence. Energy and resources continue to be directed toward more sophisticated violence. Where is the Beatitude attitude in this? We discover ourselves being held captives by our own weapons. The words of the late General Omar Bradley indict us.

We have grasped the mystery of the atom and rejected the Sermon on the Mount. The world has achieved brilliance without wisdom, power without conscience. Ours is a world of nuclear giants and ethical infants. We know more about war than we know about peace, more about killing than we know about living.[2]

Our fascination with destruction and our perception of power as the ability to destroy creation are frightening. We are in the clutches of the demonic. Whenever we choose things over people, we sin. In our grasp for security we have listened to the father of lies who has told every culture that if it had a bigger stick than any other culture it would be secure and have life the way it wanted life to be. We need to develop pride and appreciation for people who demonstrate their helpfulness with their gifts and service to fellow human beings rather than when they demonstrate hurtfulness with guns, bombs, and destructive power. Arnold Toynbee was perceptive about what is needed.

> The West has erred because it has chosen to fight Communism with Communism's own material weapons. As long as the battle is fought on these terms, the Communists will keep on winning. The West must base its appeal on more than freedom, more than prosperity; it must base its appeal on religion. Only in this way can democracy turn the tables on the Communist assailants. The grace of God might bring about this miracle.

One objective of Jesus' ministry was to liberate those who are oppressed. People the world over are oppressed when they live under the mushroom cloud threat of a nuclear winter. As people experience the liberation which Christ offers they begin hearing the invitation to be peacemakers—not *peacekeepers* but *peacemakers*. We are to create peace and this calls for initiatives by us that lead to peace. Such initiatives will be encircled by conflict because making peace is a road out of bondage which is frightening because never before have we traveled this road. Making peace is a positive, initiating action that begins by resisting destructive polarization.

Jesus' life-style signaled the liberation that occurs with making peace. By word and deed He demonstrated the stages through which the law of retaliation had passed, and how it finally came to rest in the universal love of God. The stages are unlimited retaliation, limited retaliation, limited love, and unlimited love.

In unlimited retaliation no limit is placed on revenge. If someone puts out your eye, then if at all possible you put out both of his. All is fair in unlimited retaliation. Might makes right. If you are able to inflict more injury than you receive, then you have the right to do it. The rule is: Do unto others so they cannot do unto you. Brief reflection causes many to conclude there is a better way.

Limited retaliation is a better way. Limited retaliation says that if someone knocks one of your teeth out, you can retaliate by knocking out one of his. You cannot knock out all of his teeth. In other words, get even but no more. The rule is: Do unto others as they do unto you. Limited retaliation is better than unlimited retaliation but if this rule is followed the world becomes filled with blind, toothless people.

The culture out of which the Old Testament was formed developed a better way, the way of limited love. Limited love is stated as "Love your neighbor and hate your enemy" (Matt. 5:43, also see Lev. 19:18). If a neighbor caused injury, he might be forgiven, but if an enemy caused injury, then give him the works. An enemy could be punished as harshly and as drastically as desired. In those days a neighbor was a Jew and an enemy was a Gentile. For too many of us today a neighbor is a white Anglo-Saxon Protestant and an enemy is anyone else. The rule of limited love is: Do unto your enemies as they do to you. The result is a double standard, one for people who are known and liked and another for those unknown and/or disliked.

Jesus' intention was to free people from the bondage of retaliation and limited love. His method was never to pay back evil with evil but to return good for evil, to turn the other cheek, and to go the second mile. His life-style and His instructions to disciples added up to a person permitting others to impose on him. This approach expresses unlimited love and involves loving outsiders and praying for those who try to do in others. We tend to go along with this unlimited love approach as long as the enemy is weaker than we because turning the cheek won't hurt too much. We claim this approach won't work with a bigger, stronger enemy.

An Austrian colonel told of his orders to march against a little town in the Tyrol and lay siege to it. One prisoner who had been captured said, "You'll never take that town because they have an invincible leader." No one seemed to know what the prisoner meant nor who the leader was. The colonel doubled his preparation. As they descended through the pass in the Alps, the cattle were still in the field, the women and children, and even the men were at work in the fields. An ambush was apparent. As the soldiers drew nearer the town they passed people on the road who smiled and greeted them and went on their way.

Finally, the soldiers reached the town and clattered up the street. People came to their windows and doorways. Some looked a little startled and then went on their way. The soldiers arrived at the town hall. Out came an old white-haired man followed by ten men in peasant clothes. The old man walked to the colonel and extended his hand.

"Where are your soldiers?" the colonel asked.

"Why, don't you know we have none?" the old man replied.

"But we have come to take this town," exclaimed the colonel.

"Well, no one will stop you."

"Are there none here to fight?" asked the colonel.

The old man responded, "No, there is no one here to fight. We have chosen Christ for our leader and He taught people another way."

The colonel and his soldiers left the town as they had found it. It was impossible to take it.

Our claim is that the way of unlimited love is impractical. All that happens in such an approach is that people get nailed. That is true. The road to freedom which Jesus invites us to walk is not a road to practicality by the world's standards. Jesus tells us to love our enemies because that attitude is essential if we are to create peace. Peace takes root in the soil of righteousness and is watered by mercy and forgiveness. It is easier to promote strife than to create peace. It does take two to make a quarrel, but even my most hostile antagonist cannot break the peace unless I collaborate with him. If I resolve to make peace, peace will be made.

The consuming desire of God was voiced by the angels at the birth of His son, ". . . on earth peace!" (Luke 2:14 b). God's way of making peace is not merely to cause an outward settlement between people, but to create people of goodwill. God's peace is the sober insight that sees and receives the hurt of the world, calls it what it is, warns others, and returns to the world, hoping to transform and redeem the world. The One whose birth announcement was peace grew up to be the Prince of peace. It was He who called disciples to be creators of peace and said they would be called children of God. By whom? Not by the general community of people. Not even by the majority in the church. Many, both in and out of the church, will accuse the makers of peace as being disturbers of peace because trouble will follow them wherever they go. Makers of peace will disturb the status quo by moving away from it or against it. The makers of peace will receive the barbs of hatred rather than the accolades of praise from the populace. God calls the peacemakers His children. It matters very little what people call the peacemakers. It matters greatly what God calls them.

Being Persecuted

Jesus suggested that peacemaking leads right into persecution and that leads to happiness. What a question that raises! Jesus barely had gotten His ministry underway when He uttered the Beatitudes. I wonder how much His words haunted Jesus when the Pharisees hounded Him.

Here is how Jesus said He would liberate people from oppression. He would call them to join Him as disciples. As His disciples they would need to declare spiritual bankruptcy, grieve over their condition, be open to learn from God and others, crave to do what is right, be merciful, have their focus on God, and work for peace. Then they would be doing what God requires and the result would be persecution. How ironic! What strange logic this is. We cannot let go of this eighth Beatitude. Rather it will not let us go. It grips us with intrigue and raises difficult questions.

One of the first questions is, "What is persecution?" Persecution is the act of being afflicted or harassed constantly with the intent to cause injury or distress. Persecution is cruel oppression, especially for reasons of religion, politics, or race. To be persecuted is to live in an atmosphere of suffocating suspicion, to be pursued by persons in a malignant spirit, to be sniped at by enemies lying in wait, to be hounded and harassed with unjust penalties for alleged offenses.

A second question is, "Why is this person being persecuted?" Some people live frightened, suspicious lives. They are convinced that there are other people "out there" who are attempting and succeeding in doing harm to them. Waves of suspicion continue to break on international shores in relationships between the Soviet Union and the United States. People motivated by fear urge that we live by the ungolden rule of doing to them before they do to us. The wave of suspicion breaks on our national shores as the serpents of racism and anti-Semitism raise their many heads. Such suspicion and fear become justification for hatred and violence for too many people and fuel the fires of persecution. People who are motivated to hatred and violence by fear and suspicion become the persecutors rather than the persecuted.

Being persecuted is not proof of virtue. Sadistic people gain pleasure by inflicting pain on others—both emotional and physical. Receiving the hostile, maltreatment of sadistic people does not result in the happiness to which Jesus referred. Masochistic people derive pleasure from experiencing pain—both emotional and physical. These people often provoke maltreatment and then revel in being mistreated. There are people who are unable to experience any degree of intimacy until they have caused an uproar and arrived at a victim status.

Self-pity may lead a person to persecute herself if she can't get anyone else to persecute her. The blame always is placed on someone else and it really doesn't matter what hurts the one who is suffering from self-inflicted persecution. Just so she hurts is what is important; therefore, she has a legitimate reason to feel sorry for herself. This person has to suffer for a cause, even if it's "just because."

Suppose there are people who not only oppose us but also who really are persecuting us. We should not jump to the conclusion that we are suffering for righteousness' sake. The first value of persecution is the inducement of self-examination. Our self-examination ought to include introspection in light of the other Beatitudes as well as exploring the possibilities of why others would dislike us and want to do us harm. Oscar Wilde said he did not know why a certain man hated him so because he, Wilde, had never done anything for the man.

Persecution per se is not a blessing. A person may be opposed because he is wrong, is wicked, or is simply a disturber. I suspect that more frequently a person suffers because he is wrong than because he is right. A person may be an unloving critic or a critical lover and experience persecution for either reason.

No evidence is available to support the idea that Jesus encouraged His followers to stir up a storm, or to find one brewing and make it worse so they could be persecuted. The evidence is quite the contrary. Jesus instructed His disciples against needless antagonism, encouraging them to be as wise as serpents but as harmless as doves (Matt. 10:16). They were not to force themselves on anyone; rather, if people would not hear and receive them, they were to leave that community and go to another (Matt. 10:14).

This capstone Beatitude does not say, "Happy are those who are

persecuted." That is a half-truth and half-truth often is more danger-
ous than no truth. This eighth Beatitude says, "Happy are those who
are persecuted because they do what God requires" (Matt. 5:10,
GNB). What God requires is explained in the first. seven Beatitudes.
To translate the first seven Beatitudes into our living will result in the
eighth.

We are somewhat familiar with the persecution of the first-century
Christians, especially under the Roman emperor, Nero. Occasionally
we hear of people somewhere in the world today being persecuted
because of their religious conviction. In the summer of 1968 I met
Vishnu, an East Indian, in Georgetown, Guyana. Vishnu was twenty-
four. Three years earlier he had decided to change religions, from
Hinduism to Christianity. Only after much thought and many discussions with missionaries and with his father did he make this decision.
When he returned home after being baptized he found all his possessions dumped in the front yard of his home. He had been evicted from
his family because of his commitment to Christ.

Why do Christians in the United States get off so easily compared
to first-century Christians or to Vishnu? Are unchristian citizens of
the United States that much better than unchristian Romans or unchristian East Indians? Is it that our light is so dim that the tormentor
cannot see it? What are the things we do that are worth persecuting?

As with the previous seven Beatitudes, thus it is with the eighth one
that happiness is a by-product. Jesus suggested that happiness was the
good fortune of those who receive God's salvation, but His understanding completely contradicts the ideas and values of a sensual
society that equates happiness with materialism. Often we live as
though happiness can be pursued or grasped. The faster we run after
happiness the quicker it escapes us. The tighter we clutch at happiness
when we experience it, the sooner we strangle it. Happiness, as Jesus
expressed it, is not so much bubbling effervescence as it is a state of
contentment that is evident in those who hear His words and do them.

Jesus expanded and interpreted the eighth Beatitude, no doubt,
because it was the climax and the direct result of the previous seven.
As He expanded this eighth Beatitude, Jesus personalized the application of the Beatitude by shifting from saying, "Happy are [they]," to
say "Happy are you." Jesus saw the state of contentment in His
disciples because they were His followers. The persecution they ex-

perienced and the false things said against them also were the result of being His followers.

Blessedness or happiness is the by-product of persecution when the motive for action is righteousness or justice. My all-time favorite bumper sticker reads, "If you love Jesus, do justice. Any old goose can honk." Jesus never left any doubt what would happen to His followers. He expected them to be persecuted. He did not come to make life easy but to make people great by teaching them to be servants. Those who are being persecuted because of their work for righteousness have no need to call attention to their persecution because they are seeking to be liberators like Christ who liberated them. It was clear to Jesus and it must have been clear to His most casual listener that His liberating ministry was the mortal enemy of systems built on power, greed, oppression, and falsehood, and that the two systems could never lie down together.

When the church is authentically the body of Christ, it is the conscience of society, the nation, and the world. Perhaps our alleged Christianity is condemned when it is so mild that it is not persecuted but is simply ignored. Jesus encouraged His followers to be glad in hardship and to leap for joy when persecution came because there would be a great reward for His followers. The reward is not a balancing of the books but comes from God's grace. The followers of Christ are invited into the realm of His reign because they have been faithful. Their faithfulness is actually a result of God's grace. The ability to be faithful is a gift from God.

Jesus adds that when His disciples are persecuted for doing what is right, for being merciful to others, for making peace, they are in good company. This was how Israel treated the prophets who preceded them. Bitter persecution may come to the follower of Christ because the servant is not above the Master.

The interpretation of the eighth Beatitude is concluded with a warning. "You are the salt of the earth. You are the light of the world" (Matt. 5:13 a-14 a). We want to put a period after each of these statements and receive them as compliments rather than heed them as warnings. Jesus warned, "You are the salt of the earth; but if salt has lost its taste, how shall its saltness be restored? It is no longer good for anything except to be thrown out and trodden under foot by men" (v. 13). If Jesus' followers lose their ability to set people free from spiritual poverty, injustice, greed, hunger, and war, then people will no longer persecute them. They will just dump them on the ground and go about their business.

The followers of Christ also are the light of the world. Their light is to shine, not so people can see the sanctuary, hear the choir, read the financial report, but so that others may become followers of Christ, seeking to do what God desires.

During World War II an American pastor visited Heinrich Niemoeller in Germany. Niemoeller's son Martin had been a pastor in Germany. He had defied Hitler, was put in prison, and spent several months in a concentration camp. The American pastor expressed his concern for the Niemoellers. Heinrich Niemoeller replied,

> When you go back to America do not let anyone pity the father and mother of Martin Niemoeller. Only pity any follower of Christ who does not know the joy that is set before those who endure the cross despising the shame. Yes, it is a terrible thing to have a son in a concentration camp. Paula here and I know that. But there would be something more terrible for us: if God had needed a faithful martyr and our Martin had been unwilling.

Isn't this the essence of what Jesus said? Persecution is a terrible thing, but unfaithfulness is far worse.

Many have implied that the Beatitudes make no sense by saying that followers of Christ must use common sense. They want to dilute the Beatitudes because they are not common and make no sense according to the world's mentality, but the Beatitudes of Jesus carry His ministry of liberation. Freedom from spiritual poverty begins with recognizing the need. Freedom from bitterness and resentment comes through grief work. Only the teachable can be liberated from ignorance which will lead to an insatiable appetite for righteousness. Giving mercy frees one from rigidity and enables one to create peace which produces a state of contentment undergirding a disciple in the midst of persecution. Jesus' ministry of liberation produces freedom and faithfulness.

The Recovery of Sight

When Jesus said that part of His ministry included the recovery of sight to the blind, evidently He was referring to His desire and intention to bring wholeness to the total person. Jesus knew that sight recovery involved more than the regeneration of optical nerves. He enabled some to see who had been physically blind, but there were plenty of people who had good eyesight but poor vision. The religious leaders were the worst. Often the same is true today. Religious leaders frequently have poor vision or no vision. Jesus referred to the Pharisees as blind leaders of the blind (Matt. 15:14). Certainly Jesus wanted these to recover their vision just as much as He wanted the blind to recover their sight.

As Luke suggested, there were temptations for Jesus beyond His forty-day wilderness experience. Certainly His ministry was fraught with temptations such as His temptations to be a miracle man, to be conservative, and to seek safety.

The Temptation to Be a Miracle Man

The healing which Jesus brought to the diseased and disabled was viewed with amazement and interpreted by most as miraculous. These situations created difficulties for Jesus as they increased His popularity, causing people to flock to Him for what they could get out of Him. This dimension of ministry also placed Jesus in the middle of tension between being a miracle man and being the Messiah. The option to be a miracle man was offered first in the wilderness when Jesus considered turning stones into bread. Although the sensational of today becomes the commonplace of tomorrow, the temptation to be sensational remains. That temptation continued to tug at Jesus throughout His ministry.

Whenever Jesus did anything that was interpreted as miraculous, the risk was that the event would be used sensationally. Much of the contemporary struggle with miracles is the tendency to have a dictionary definition of miracle rather than its biblical usage. *Miracle* is defined in a dictionary as an event or action that apparently contradicts known scientific laws and is thought to be due to supernatural causes.

In biblical writings a miracle is not something contrary to nature. Healing is the restoration of a natural function rather than an extraordinary event. The miracle lies in the fact that through an event God reveals Himself in His gracious activity to the eyes of a believer. Every event that is identified as a miracle is open to other interpretations. A nonbeliever can see the same event as a believer, seeing nothing of God disclosed and see no miracle. Matthew expressed this concept when he wrote "Because they had no faith, he performed no miracles

(13:58, author). Miracles are not for nonbelievers and their purpose
is not to convert nonbelievers to believers. Miracles are windows that
open to the inner side of people's existence where God reveals His
providential guidance.[3]

A person who believes in God will believe in the possibility of
miracles, which are a variety of events in and through which one sees
an act, revelation, or disclosure of God. Belief in miracles presupposes
belief in God, but a person's trust in God is not contingent upon one
or more miraculous events.

There were times when Jesus' disciples were unclear about who He
was. After He had calmed a storm they marveled at Him and wondered aloud who this was that even the wind obeyed (Mark 4:41). As
His fame spread (Mark 1:28) and as people sought an audience with
Him (v. 37) the temptation was with Jesus to play to the gallery.
Matthew 16:1-4 and Mark 8:11-13 record the request of a miracle
made by the Pharisees. Their claim was that this would prove to them
that God approved of Jesus. Jesus refused to play their game and
pointed out that if they could not see the evidence readily available
to them neither would they see an additional sign by Him.

Even in His last moments the temptation was there for Him to do
the spectacular in response to the promise by those in the crowd to
believe in Him if He would save Himself (Mark 15:29-31). Luke told
of one of the thieves expressing the same temptation (Luke 23:39).
The temptation for Jesus to be a miracle man rather than a Messiah
continually was before Him all the way to the end of His life.

The Temptation to Be Conservative

Jesus dared to be radical in the original meaning of the term.
Radical comes from the Latin *radix* and means "root." Jesus sought
to go to the root or heart of an issue. The temptation to maintain the
status quo, stay the course, relate to people on the basis of appearance
remained before Jesus. But He dared to be radical by relating to
people on the basis of human need.

There are numerous examples of radicality in Jesus' ministry. Jesus
touched a leper (Mark 1:4) which made Him ceremonially unclean.
He healed a paralytic (Mark 2:5) and announced that his sins were
forgiven. Jesus not only associated with tax-collectors but also called
one to be His disciple (Mark 2:14). Later He had lunch with Zacchaeus (Luke 19:1-5). Jesus' disciples picked grain on the sabbath (Mark

2:23-28). He dared to relate to the demoniac rather than shun him as others did (Mark 5:1-20). A woman who suffered from hemorrhaging touched Jesus in a crowd (5:25-34). Such an encounter made Jesus unclean according to the religious law of His people. Jesus resisted the temptation to be conservative with regard to the cleanliness laws (Mark 7:1-23). Jesus' radicality is in bold relief in His relationship with women (Mark 1:30-31; 5:29-34; 7:24-30; 10:1-12; 12:41-44; 14:3-9; 15:40-41; 16:1-8; John 4:1-30; John 8:1-11).

Jesus and the Sabbath

The Ten Commandments were the guidelines for Judaism. Through the years questions were raised about the application of those guidelines. Rabbis in giving interpretations developed more than six hundred rules to interpret the guidelines. Devotion to God was primary and it was demonstrated by worship and rest on the sabbath. A list of permissible and unpermissible sabbath activities was developed. No work was permitted on the sabbath and distance walking was work. Thus the sabbath day's journey developed, the limit of which was a mile. Plucking heads of grain was considered harvesting and was not permitted. Jesus' disciples were guilty of breaking the sabbath.

Jesus made a radical statement that got to the heart or root of the issue. "The sabbath was made for man and not man for the sabbath" (Mark 2:27). The sabbath had become an institution. Every institution, including the church, is to serve people. No institution is sacred, but people are. The sabbath had come to be treated as sacred in Jesus' day and the Pharisees were tempting Him to be conservative by staying the course of the sabbath sanctity which had become more important than people. The sanctity that any institution deserves is derived from the service it gives to the broad spectrum of human needs. Jesus resisted the temptation to be conservative and dared to be radical with His statement about the sabbath.

Jesus and Cleanliness

Jesus' encounter with the scribes and Pharisees over the issue of handwashing is very revealing. Jesus' desire to bring the recovery of sight to the blind was likewise relevant. These religious leaders saw the little things but they were blind to the big things. They noted if people washed their hands before they ate. My mother used to take notice of that, too, but she didn't conclude that I was impure to worship God because I had not washed my hands. The Pharisees had become so meticulous about hand washing and pot scrubbing that they could not see how people were relating to each other and to God or the significance of those relationships. The Pharisees usually failed to take an open look at Jesus and His teachings. Their eyes were blind to everything except their customs and authority.

Religion had become such an external matter, but Jesus made it an internal one. He radically stated that nothing outside of a person could either defile or purify. What comes from the inwardness of people is what reveals their purity or their defilement.

The Pharisees were challenging and tempting Jesus to conserve their traditions for the sake of the traditions. Whenever Jesus was confronted with the options of things or people He chose people every time. It was Jesus' hope that the Pharisees would recover their sight when He dared to be radical, but they chose to remain blind.

Jesus and Women

Perhaps the most radical stance Jesus took was His relationship with women. The fact that He publicly related to women was radical in itself. In that culture women were property. They were treated as things, but Jesus elevated women to the place of equality with men. John records two of the most radical things Jesus did and both of them involve women (John 4:1-30; John 8:1-11). In the first passage John tells about Jesus' conversation with the Samaritan woman at the well. Jesus was radical on three counts: He talked to a Samaritan, He talked to a woman, and He talked to her in public. So intense was the hatred and bitterness between the Jews and Samaritans that often Jews traveling between Judea and Galilee would walk up the eastern side of the Jordan River rather than walk through Samaria.

Not only did Jesus talk openly with a woman but also He as a Jew asked to drink from the "unclean" bucket of a Samaritan. In addition, the woman's marital status categorized her as a sinful woman which is additional evidence of Jesus' radicality. What astonished Jesus' disciples was that He talked with a woman in public. That was even more unconventional given the facts that He was a rabbi and she was a Samaritan. Here, as always, Jesus perceived and related to a person as a person, and this woman was challenged by Jesus to become a person before she sought to be anything else.

Although the passage in John 7:53 to 8:11 does not appear in the oldest and best manuscripts, the story rings true to what is otherwise known about Jesus. Jesus was in the Temple area teaching when scribes and Pharisees brought a woman to Jesus who had been caught in adultery. They reminded Jesus of Moses' law and asked what He thought ought to be done. Jesus did not reply immediately; rather, He doodled in the sand. It is impossible to know what, if anything, He wrote in the sand. Perhaps His action gave the woman time to realize that her accusers were after Jesus as well as her. (I wonder why the man caught in adultery was not brought to Jesus.) The scribes and Pharisees saw this woman as a worthless object they could use to trap Jesus.

No doubt these religious leaders were getting antsy with what they interpreted as a mere delaying tactic by Jesus. Finally Jesus stood up and said, "Let him who is without sin among you be the first to throw a stone at her" (John 8:7). Jesus doodled in the sand some more. He had not condoned adultery but He had compelled the religious leaders to judge themselves. None of them could pass the test and they slipped away quietly, one by one, until only Jesus and the woman were left. He asked her, "Woman, where are they? Has no one condemned you?" She said, "No one, Lord," and Jesus said "Neither do I condemn you; go and do not sin again" (John 8:10-11). Jesus acknowledged that the woman had sinned, and He turned her in a new direction.

Jesus was tempted to be conservative. This text in John says the leaders came to test Jesus. They were tempting Jesus to conserve the law of Moses regardless of what that did to this person they were using. The religious leaders were blind to this woman as a person and saw her only as an object they could use. Jesus dared to be radical. He saw her as a person and sought to aid her in recovering her ability to see herself as a person of worth. This woman was challenged to a new self-awareness and a new life because Jesus resisted the temptation to be conservative and sought to be radical, to get at the root of the issue—to relate to this woman as a person of worth. There is no indication that the religious leaders recovered their sight. The evidence is that their vision worsened because they continued to plot ways to destroy Jesus.

The Temptation to Seek Safety

Jesus was not long into His ministry before He began experiencing resistance and opposition. As Luke told it, opposition began to mount before Jesus even left the synagogue in Nazareth. Jesus' early opposition came from the religious establishment, primarily from many of the scribes and Pharisees. The populace swarmed to Jesus. He spoke with such freshness, reached through the barriers that separated them from others, and touched their pain and suffering. No doubt jealousy was a contributing factor to the religious leaders' opposition to Jesus. But an even more significant factor was Jesus' apparent disregard for all the traditions and customs that helped them know who they were and to know they were righteous, even if it were self-righteous. Jesus threatened their security and they, in turn, threatened His.

I have yet to meet a healthy person who thrived on having adversaries. I get no hints in the Gospels that Jesus enjoyed being embroiled in conflict with the religious leaders. Since part of His task was to bring recovery of sight to the blind, the religious leaders were some of the ones to whom He hoped to minister. In many ways Jesus became embattled because the religious leaders countered Him at every point whether He had healed a paralytic (Mark 2:10), ate with tax collectors and sinners (v. 16), or healed a man on the sabbath (Mark 3:5).

It is evident from Jesus' dialogue with the religious leaders that He wanted to cooperate with them. He asked which was easier—to forgive sins or to say "Rise, take up your pallet and go home" (Mark 2:11). He asked other leaders if it were lawful to do good or harm on the sabbath (Mark 3:4). Was He not stating that He wanted them to join Him in working for the benefit of people? Surely He was tempted to compromise His commitment in order to reduce opposition and to play it safe.

Jesus' security was not in any great danger as long as His opposition was only religious. Political authorities would not permit a skirmish to get out of control. However, when the religious leaders teamed up with the political leaders, Jesus' life was in danger (Mark 3:6).

Perhaps the sign which indicated Jesus' fate was the death of John the Baptist. He was beheaded by Herod. Jesus had been billed as greater than John; He may have expected even worse things for Himself. John the Baptist had dared to speak to Herod about the wrongness of his marriage and was imprisoned as a result. The beheading came as a request from Herodias through her daughter.

Jesus obviously was shocked by the event. "Now when Jesus heard this, he withdrew from there in a boat to a lonely place apart" (Matt. 14:13). Jesus had been making some stern statements. Perhaps He should tone down His comments, be more cautious about what He said. Is there any reason why such thoughts may have run through His mind?

The temptation to seek safety was spoken clearly by Jesus' disciples. As Jesus looked out on the horizon of His life, He saw His path and that of the religious leaders on a collision course. He expressed His concern to His disciples, and Peter immediately insisted that would not happen. Right then Jesus was possibly tempted to ask for Peter's ideas on how He could seek safety. Instead, He confronted Peter by calling him the obstructor and telling him to get behind Him.

Later when Jesus was on the mount of transfiguration with Peter, James, and John, Peter suggested they just stay on the mountain. They had had such a rich experience there, they were out of the fray of the crowds, and they could avoid confrontations with the religious and political leadership by staying there. It really was a safe harbor, but Jesus refused to take it, not because He was eager to get Himself killed but because He unwilling to compromise His commitment.

The most agonizing time Jesus had in being tempted to seek safety was in the garden of Gethsemane. While there He knew that a direct confrontation was at hand and He wanted to avoid it if possible. He prayed that all things were possible with God. Certainly one of the possibilities was that He could slip off in the night or He could cut a deal with the authorities. Three times He prayed that the cup pass from Him. Is this not evidence that Jesus was wrestling with the temptation to seek security? But He did not give in to the temptation. He saw this temptation to seek security as blindness, and He came to restore sight, not to diminish or destroy it.

As Jesus sought to restore sight to the blind He encountered some of His greatest resistance and opposition. It was true then and now that there are none so blind as those who will not see. Some of the Pharisees were blind leaders of the blind. Jesus was so radical, so unconventional to them that they felt threatened and enraged. In His confrontations with the religious leaders, Jesus was tempted to be a miracle man rather than the Messiah, to be conservative rather than radical, and to trade His commitment for safety and security.

To Proclaim the Acceptable
Year of the Lord

In my early teenage years, late one night a strange cracking sound caught the attention of my family. We looked across the street from our front door. Approximately fifteen feet above the ground was a strange fuse-like flame that seemed to burn but neither increase nor diminish. Mother turned to Dad and asked, "Do you think this is the end of time?" Soon the fire trucks came and it was determined that an electrical wire was shorting out, causing the flame.

The fear of the unknown focuses in a variety of ways for us. Ultimate fear of the unknown is death and this fear is intensified for many with their belief in an instantly catastrophic end of the universe. More often than not verbalization of this fear is expressed by strong emotional woes and warnings to people of the horrible destruction that God is going to rain upon the earth. The fear of the unknown is turned into a source of motivation by which people, driven by fear, are encouraged to turn their lives in another direction.

Fear of the unknown was not a source of motivation that Jesus used to gain followers. Certainly Jesus confronted people with whom they were and whom they could be. His sternest challenges and strongest judgments were leveled against the religious leaders of His day but even those encounters did not have the venom that comes from many pulpits today. Jesus was seeking to proclaim the acceptable year of the Lord rather than the celebrated demise of those who had ears but would not hear.

Much emphasis has been placed on the *eschaton,* the end of time. During a time of turbulence within a culture there is heightened hysteria and a morbid curiosity about the last things. Every age has crises and every crisis breeds counterfeit leaders who for their own gain exploit humanity's widespread fear.

Our fear is intensified now that human beings have the ability to destroy the entire world and all future generations in a nuclear holocaust. We have the ability to erase the human species but we do not have the authority. Such ability heightens tensions and many equate such potentially lethal actions with the workings of God, but it is not true. The God of the Bible is the Creator not the discreator, the

Constructor not the destructor. The problems of life overwhelm us and we want to wrap up in a cocoonlike existence expressing our desires like the leading man in the movie *Silkwood* who said, "Just give me problems that I can solve."

Thus people through the ages have sought to deal with the problems of change, turbulency, and cultural upheaval by giving their fear and anxiety a religious interpretation and claiming that God is getting ready to destroy the world. Nothing seems further from the understanding of Jesus about the nature and intentions of God. How could such destruction and even glee with which some anticipate it be the acceptable year of the Lord?

The acceptable year of the Lord is a biblical phrase that identifies the dawning of the age of salvation. Jesus felt strongly about the significance of His present time as the time when the kingdom of God and salvation were at the point of arriving (Luke 12:54-56). Then and now there were those who wanted to interpret the current events as signs that God was in desperation and exasperation and had given up on creation. Jesus warned against such interpretations. Preoccupation with the end of the age leads astray. G.K. Chesterton said there are many people who know the last word about everything and the first word about nothing.[4]

During Jesus' ministry there were those concerned about the end of time and speculated about it. The Pharisees sought signs, even when signs were all around them (Matt. 12:38ff.). They had in mind the signs of God's activity according to what they understood to be signs. Jesus warned that preoccupation with the end of the age or the end of time was futile because only God knows those things (Matt. 24:36). In our day we ought to be less concerned about knowing when the end of the age will come because one of the main contributions of our increased technology and knowledge is that we know so very little compared to what we don't know. In one sense we know more and more about less and less.

We ought to take a hint from Jesus about sign reading. Jesus illustrated God's activity in the events of His day with a fig tree (vv. 32-35). The fig tree was not a tragic figure; rather, the description Jesus gave of the fig tree illustrates hope. The leaves sprouting forth on the tree reveal that summer is not far away and signify the beginning of new growth.

The fig tree lesson is set in the context of troubles, persecutions, and great difficulties for the followers of Christ and the agony that the end time will be. Why the agony? Because people have not prepared for it. They have followed after false gods and false messiahs. Proclaiming the age of salvation or the year of the Lord's favor is the natural logical consequence and culmination of proclaiming good news to the poor, release to the captives, and recovery of sight to the blind. Those who receive the good news are freed from bondage, regain their sight, and enter into the age of salvation. Is this not a fitting climax to the ministry in which Jesus was engaged?

Ministry that proclaims good news to the poor, liberation to the captives, and the recovery of sight to the blind results in proclaiming the acceptable year of the Lord. This ministry will protect us from focusing on schedules, timetables, charts, and clocks trying to pinpoint when Christ will return. The Bible affirms both the certainty that Christ will return and the clear uncertainty when this will occur. When events are extremely complex and we feel a keen sense of complete helplessness, we clamor for certainty and security. Many see that security resting in the near future with God intervening and ending the entire enterprise of creation. We prefer that someone very strong would swoop in and solve all of our problems, delivering us from the necessity of responsible involvement.

Conclusion

The Sermon on the Mount is the sermon of sermons. It is Jesus' liberation manifesto. Jesus' objective in His ministry was redemption, setting people free from what oppressed and captivated them. The Beatitudes describe the liberating process for one being redeemed. Thus the Beatitudes are the redeeming words of Jesus. Our release from bondage begins with our admission of being spiritually bankrupt. That leads us to mourn for ourselves and for others through which we find comfort. Then we are open to be teachable. When we are teachable we hunger for righteousness, we seek to be merciful, develop pure hearts, make peace, and are willing to experience persecution because we are learning what liberation genuinely means and what it means to be ministers of liberation. The redeeming words of Christ take root in us and bear fruit through our liberating encounters with others.

Jesus was tempted in a variety of ways to be diverted from His ministry of redemption. But Jesus refused to allow the pleas or signs or the speculations about the end of the age to obstruct Him from His objectives to proclaim good news to the poor, release to the captives, and recovery of sight to the blind. For Jesus to accomplish these three objectives resulted in His fourth objective, proclaiming the acceptable year of the Lord. The redeeming words of Jesus are lasting words because His words invite us to a lasting ministry. If we will focus on the first things as Jesus did, then we will not become preoccupied and diverted by the last things. We will discover that to proclaim good news to the poor, release to the captives, and recovery of sight to the blind is to proclaim the acceptable year of the Lord.

Notes

1. Mary Cosby, Speech given to the Ministers' Conference of the District of Columbia Baptist Convention, December 8, 1983.

2. Recorded in *Baptist Peacemaker,* Vol. 1, No. 1, December 1980, p. 1. Published by Deer Park Baptist Church, Louisville, Ky.

3. E. Glenn Hinson, *The Reaffirmation of Prayer* (Nashville: Broadman Press, 1979), pp. 107-108.

4. George A. Buttrick, ed., *The Interpreter's Bible Commentary* (Nashville: Abingdon Press, 1957), Vol. 7, p. 856.

5

The Last Words of Jesus

John 10:17-18

When a person's life has ended, it is natural for us to remember the last words the deceased said to us. This is a means of retaining our kinship with the person and underscoring his importance to us. Although several people hear the same words, everyone does not remember and recount the same words. This is how it is with the last words of Christ. Seven statements are attributed to Christ as having been spoken from the cross. Not one of the Gospel writers recorded all seven statements. Is it any wonder? Consider all that was occurring. Those who had been closest to Christ seemed far away at this point. It is as if they were going away from the cross looking back over their shoulders. They were drawn to and repulsed from the cross simultaneously. How could they hear anything?

The words Jesus spoke from the cross reveal the temptations He experienced in the last hours of His life and how He responded to those temptations. Jesus' last words have multiple meanings and implications for us. They are lasting words not only because they tell us how Christ died but also because they tell us how to die. How a person dies is related to how he lives. Never was this more clearly evident than in the living and dying of Jesus the Christ. Thus His last words have lasting value for us.

Father, Forgive Them:
Luke 23:34

Much earlier, when the disciples had asked Jesus to teach them to pray, He said, "Say, . . . 'Father.' " Jesus' use of this simple address, "Father," represented a significant practice and teaching of Jesus. Judaism already knew God as Father, but the direct, warm, personal, childlike address, "Abba," represented something new. *Abba* is Aramaic for *father*. This was a child's way of addressing his father, almost like our word, *Dad*. Jesus' address to God as "Abba, Father" (Mark 14:36) was a simple, affectionate approach to God. Such an address reflected the closeness and warmth Jesus felt toward God. Jesus knew God as "Dad" and He came to enable us to know Him that way. Thus, Jesus taught His disciples to call upon God using "Abba." Probably the early Christians used *Abba* as their own word for *Father* when they addressed God.[1] This use of *Abba* by Jesus expressed His intimacy with God, but it does not imply a banal self-assurance of taking the relationship for granted.[2]

What Jesus taught, He practiced and experienced Himself. Intimacy between persons goes beyond a theoretical discussion; it is a love relationship. This is what Jesus taught in the Model Prayer. He taught His disciples to be able to relate to God as a loving parent as a natural outgrowth of an intimate love relationship with God. Jesus had nurtured the intimate relationship that had begun early in His life when He said, "Wist ye not that I must be about my Father's business?" (Lke 2:49, KJV). He found that relationship to be sustaining. At His baptism he experienced the acceptance and approval of His Father: "Thou art my beloved Son, in whom I am well pleased" (Mark 1:11, KJV).

The Father was with Jesus in childhood, at His baptism, in the wilderness, in His ministry, and in the garden of Gethsemane. Jesus' prayer in Gethsemane is evidence that Jesus prayed the way He taught His disciples to pray. There, in the agony of decision making, He put words to His struggle and it came out, "Dad, Father, I pray this cup might pass from me (Mark 14:36, Author).

It should not surprise us that Jesus' first last word is "Father," but it does. Perhaps it is the events between "Father" in the garden and "Father" from the cross that shock us. Think of the intensity of life for Jesus during the twelve-hour period preceding His crucifixion. He had gone to supper with friends, relived the Exodus of His people, agonized in prayer, was betrayed, arrested, denied, tried, condemned, and walked up the hill to His death. With His body still in agony from the scourging and the jolt of his executioners dropping the cross in place, with death imminent, Jesus called out, "Father." Jesus' life is evidence that the attitude a person has about life and living contributes significantly to his attitude about death and dying. The relationship Jesus had with His Father sustained Him in living and undergirded Him in dying.

The real jolt in Jesus' prayer from the cross was not, "Father," but "Forgive them." Who did He want forgiven? "Them" was inclusive. Jesus may have been including the people who watched, the rulers who scoffed, the soldiers who gambled, and the disciples who scattered. But how could He ask forgiveness for those who turned Him in, for those who did Him in, for those who left Him alone, and for those who cheered on the executioners?

How could He pray, "Forgive them"? Perhaps, because, in Gethsemane, He had prayed for Himself and found resolution for the turmoil, agony, and struggle within Himself, so that now He could pray for others, "Father, forgive them." But these words were shocking. Several of the important, early manuscripts did not record these words.[3] The words were difficult for the early church. For a man being crucified to cry, "Father, forgive them," was just too much.

Some early Christians could not stand His forgiving the Jews in this way. In Acts 4:10 the Jews are accused of the crucifixion of Christ in the second and third centuries which may explain why manuscripts like Papyrus 75, Codex Vaticanus, and Codex Bezae do not have Jesus offering this forgiveness. However, the persecuted church let these words stand in the best manuscripts such as Sinaiticus and Alexandrinus. Many preferred revenge to reconciliation. There were those in the church in the early years who did not want Jesus forgiving Jews, Romans, Samaritans, criminals, prostitutes, or tax-collectors. This is so contemporary. There are those today who don't like Jesus being so forgiving. But, the church let the words stand in the best manuscripts, for these words say something radically significant about Christ and those who follow Him.

When Jesus cried, "Father, forgive them," He sided with people. Having sought to build a bridge to people throughout His ministry, Jesus continued His work of reconciliation even when the worst was done to Him. In an early chapter of Matthew, Jesus joined people in need, adding His strength to theirs, "seeing them with every illness and disease, he was moved with compassion!" (Matt. 9:35-36, Author) Later, He wept for Jerusalem. In this cry, "Father, forgive them," He joined Jerusalem. When Jerusalem would not come to Him, He went to Jerusalem. By going to Jerusalem, He stepped over the wall that separated, and demonstrated how far the love of God extends. Even at the very doorway of death, Jesus expressed this love. His expression was not a live-and-let live philosophy nor an insipid "let bygones be bygones." Neither did Jesus mean forgetting and smiling, nor understanding and saying, "They are worth it." Jesus was offering forgiveness, not sentimentality.

Why was Jesus requesting forgiveness for those who were not seeking it themselves? When a wrong is done, the wrongdoer has separated himself from the one wronged. Strange as it seems, the quickest and healthiest forgiveness occurs when the one wronged initiates reconciliation. This is a paradox. Jesus embraced those who were doing Him in when He prayed, "Father, forgive them." Even in this darkest hour Jesus chose to light the candle of reconciliation rather than to curse the darkness of injustice. Jesus' approach was a great reversal. He offered forgiveness to people who had not repented because He saw forgiveness fueling repentance rather than repentance igniting forgiveness.

There are yet more words in these first of the last words of Jesus. "Father, forgive them; for they know not what they do." Does this confirm that ignorance is bliss? Are people better off not knowing? Was Jesus saying that people are better off not knowing? Was Jesus saying that people are better off not knowing because they are unaccountable for what they do not know? God forbid! Whether the unknowing, misknowing, or not knowing be a circumstantial ignorance, as with the soldiers, a judicial ignorance, of which the Jews were responsible, or a willful ignorance, as with us, the pathos of the situation here is that all are what Nicholas of Cusa called doctors of ignorance.[4] Have not all of us received our Ph.D.'s in not knowing?

When Jesus cried, "Father, forgive them; for they know not what they do," He expressed His desire for people to be forgiven, whatever their condition. They did not have to go to Him first; He came to them. Forgiveness fuels repentance. Thus, He prayed for the watching crowd, the gambling soldiers, the scoffing leaders, and the scattering disciples when He said, "Father, forgive them." We also are watchers, gamblers, and scoffers about whom He spoke and for whom He pled, "Father, forgive all of these who have their Ph.D's in unknowing." Before we realize our need for forgiveness, He already is seeking to forgive us. No one is excluded from God's forgiveness. In the life and death of His Son, God has demonstrated that He is on our side.

Jesus died as He lived. He taught His followers to pray, "[Father], forgive us our debts, As we also have forgiven our debtors" (Matt. 6:12). Jesus said to the paralytic, "Your sins are forgiven you." The same Jesus responded to the adulteress, "Neither do I condemn you; go and do not again sin" (John 8:11). And to Zaccheus, "Come down from your perch and let's have lunch together" (Luke 19:5, Author). It was Jesus who said, "Blessed are the merciful for they shall obtain mercy" (Matt. 5:7). "Turn the other cheek." "Go the second mile." "Give your cloak and coat as well." "Pray for your enemies. Do good to those who hate you" (Matt. 5:39-44, Author). Thus, the first of His last words gave expression to the attitude He had toward life and living, toward death and dying. He took his stand with humanity. Here He can be seen for who He was. He came to show that God is on our side.

People can return the favor by joining Him, or they can gamble for the leftovers. There are people who have been attending Christian churches for years who go out taking all they brought. They have come to the drama to observe, to watch. They have resisted in every way becoming a participant in this drama of dramas, the drama of redemption. They go out taking all they brought. They go out, "part his raiment and cast lots." This last word of Jesus, "Father, forgive them," is lost on them. They go out not knowing what they are doing.

Today You Will Be with Me:
Luke 23:43

Only Luke recorded the dialogue of Jesus and the repentant thief. Matthew and Mark reported that both thieves treated Jesus with the same mockery as did the rulers and the people. "And the robbers who were crucified with him also reviled him in the same way" (Matt. 27:44). Unlike His wilderness temptations, Jesus told nothing about the temptations on the cross. Was He not tempted to hurl abuse at abuse? If He could not get back at someone, could He not at least get even with somebody in the crowd or one of the thieves? He who had called and worked so hard for justice was receiving no justice. Was He not tempted to scream, "Unfair!"? Is the silence of Jesus at this point as portrayed by Matthew and Mark a quiet, reviling silence?

Characteristic of Luke's information about Jesus is how often he portrayed Jesus' identification with the outcasts: lepers, Samaritans, adulteresses, and here, a common thief. This common thief's words seem to focus our attention on the crosses and on the cross. To view the cross in the context of the words, "Today you will be with Me," affects our perception of the cross.

To look at the cross requires that we see the other crosses. There is never just one cross. Always there are other crosses. The Gospels are branded by the sight of these other crosses. Each writer tells part and parcel of the life and times of Christ, but all are equally impressed by the other crosses. The other crosses keep saying that there are times, even in this plush world of wickedness, when wickedness is punished. Malefactors sometimes are crucified. According to our view and standards, people do sometimes get just what they deserve. Malefactors as well as Saviors are crucified. Thus, there is never, and never has been, just one cross. There are many crosses, all kinds of crosses.

But what about *the* cross, Christ's cross? Why do we focus on it? What difference is there in His cross? The other crosses made no difference. They were the instruments which the law used to break people who broke the law. *The* cross itself was made like other crosses, but the *One* on the cross made the difference. The total event of Jesus' life, death, and resurrection is what made the difference. Who Jesus was made Him the Savior, not what was done to Him. It was He who said, "So there shall be one flock, one shepherd. For this reason the Father loves me, because I lay down my life, that I may take it again. No one takes it from me, but I lay it down of my own accord" (John 10:17-18). In this drama of dramas, Jesus literally died in place of Barabbas. In essence God said, "Give me Barabbas," because God always is seeking to set free the captives. Here we see that the battle is not for one person or for a segment of the population, but for all people everywhere. Christ came to all people. The whole human race is involved. No one is excluded.

Probably we could understand Jesus' identifying with His mother, or with John or one of the other disciples who had been with Him and cared about Him. But what happened is difficult for us to comprehend. It is really a simple event—so simple that all humanity nearly missed it. All that John tells is that "There they crucified him, and with him two others, one on either side, and Jesus between them" (John 19:18). Matthew and Mark add a little more, but in what they add, they treat both others alike. Without Luke, we would have missed something very significant.

The two thieves were brought along to get their executions over with on the same day. It was a matter of expediency. If they were going to kill one person, what was it to kill a couple more at the same time? The thieves watched Jesus being crucified. They waited their turns. Their anxieties rose; terror mounted. According to Luke, one of them joined the railings, "Are you not the Christ? Save yourself and us!" (Luke 23:39). Then, a human being with a terrible reputation responded to his chance. He recognized the King he had ignored. He reacted to the railing coming from his companion's cross. "Do you not fear God?" He recognized his own guilt and cried out, "We receive the due reward for our deeds." He saw something new in Jesus Christ and said, "This man has done nothing wrong." As a result of his vision, faith dawned and he cried from his cross to the center cross, "Lord, remember me when you come into your kingdom." And Jesus went all the way to the dying criminal and made a direct promise, "Today you will be with me in Paradise" (vv. 40-43). Only Luke tells of the dialogue between Jesus and this common criminal.

The structure of the cross of Christ was no different than the thief's cross. It was made of two pieces of wood like the thief's. But there was something about the way the One on that central cross turned on the lights for this one who also was dying. Maybe it was what and how he heard Jesus say, "Father, forgive them." Luke does not comment about what turned the midnight of this man's soul into the dawn of faith, but evidently forgiveness ignited repentance.

Whatever caused it, the response of the dying thief surprises us. Does this not tell us that God's kingdom always has been made up of people who are hopeless? What more hopeless person has there ever been than this criminal? He had broken the law, and now he was experiencing the consequences. What chance had he? He had no time to live a holy life. He could not learn the Lord's Prayer. He could not become a church member or be baptized or take the Lord's Supper. Of all the hopeless people you ever saw, this one is most hopeless. But any person, no matter how hopeless or how low, is acceptable to God.

Jesus identified Himself once with a paralytic to show that the loathsome might come; with a Pharisee to show that anybody could come; with a little child to show how all have to come. And here Jesus identified with this thief to show that anyone may come. Jesus was never so wrapped in Himself or so embroiled by the hurt and injustice done to Him that He could not respond to the expressed need of anyone of any status. Having been a wounded healer in His living, He also could be one in His dying. He could respond to the one who tore away His pretension and said, "We are getting what we deserve" (v. 41, GNB).

Here is the central incident of this drama at the cross. The thief cries, "Lord, keep me in mind." Christ answers, "[This very] day you will be with me in Paradise" (v. 43). The word *paradise* is a Persian word. Its root meaning is "walled garden." When a Persian king wished to do one of his subjects a very special honor, he made him a companion of the garden and he was chosen to walk in the garden with the king. The word was just beginning to be used in Palestine.[5] Jesus used the word in the sense that the dead are brought immediately into the presence of the Eternal. Jesus promised the thief the honored place of companionship in His presence. Jesus said to this common criminal that that very day He and the criminal would have the same relationship in the presence of God. Given what this man had done with his life and the immanence of his death, does he not represent human hopelessness? There was none farther away than this one, and yet Jesus went all the way to him and embraced him with the loving words, "Today you will be with Me in Paradise."

The last words of Christ are potent with meaning and intensity. They confirm that one person, *The Person,* died like He lived. These words tell us that the kingdom of God is made up of people who are hopeless. Here a hopeless human being with life fading from him caught enough of a glimpse of the Man on the center cross for the dawn of faith to break into his life. When the lights were going out, the Light came on for this common thief. This common criminal's last words were, "[Lord], remember me when you come into your kingdom" (v. 42). Jesus' last words to him were, "Today you will be with Me in Paradise." What greater promise could we desire from Christ than these same words, "Today you will be with Me. . . ."

Behold Your Mother:
John 19:25-27

Each word from the cross we examine moves us closer to the cross. There was some comfort when we were out in the crowd and He said, "Father, forgive them." At least we were lost in the crowd. No names were called. When Jesus spoke to the common criminal, "Today you will be with Me," we could hold that at a distance by being middle-class spectators. None of us are common criminals, are we?

But when He said, "Behold, your mother," Jesus got very close to home. We hear and feel the agony of family members, a mother and a son being separated. We can feel the ache because we have been

separated from a parent, or a child, or a grandparent. The reality of
the cross is stark and cold, and the ache is deep. What was this like
for Mary? With life fleeing so fast, how could Jesus be conscious of
who was there? Exploration of these questions brings us closer to the
cross, closer than we wish to be.

We know very little about the women at the cross. We know little
of what life had been like for them, and less of what effect the events
of life had had upon them. Of the three or four women who were
there, we know that Mary, the mother of Jesus, had a rough time of
it. Life had not turned out as she had expected. On this day all of her
life may have flashed before her. Her adolescent visions of life had
been filled with joy, laughter, blissful living. She had met the right
man for her life. They had plans and dreams and hopes. How different
life had been from her adolescent vision of womanhood! Would we not
all confess that life has been quite different from what we anticipated?

Certainly this was true for Mary, and it all began with the message
she received that she was "favored" of God. Luke says that Mary was
troubled by the message and wondered what the words meant. She
was young and inexperienced in living. She was engaged. When she
learned she was pregnant, she had to tell Joseph, but what would he
say? What would he do? Whatever he said or did, she could not blame
him for his feelings. Joseph began making plans to break the engage-
ment privately. Suddenly, overnight, life was going in a different
direction than Mary had anticipated. In the meantime, Joseph received a message from God. Then, the wedding was on again.

Sometime during the pregnancy, the census law went into effect.
Joseph had to go to Bethlehem to register. Mary did not have to go.
She should not go—she was carrying a baby. But Joseph did not want
to leave her, and Mary did not want to be left. It was difficult enough
to listen to the wagging tongues and see the contempt-filled eyes of
the people of Nazareth with Joseph at her side. It would be more
painful alone. Joseph wasn't about to leave Mary in such a lion's den,
and Mary wasn't interested in staying, even if she had to walk every
step of the seventy miles to Bethlehem. You know many of the events
surrounding the birth of Mary's first child. Luke summarizes these
events, "But Mary kept all these things, pondering them in her heart"
(2:19).

We don't know what of all this, if anything, Mary told Jesus. There
is no way to determine how this affected Mary and Joseph consciously

and unconsciously in their relationship to Jesus. Perhaps her love and appreciation for Joseph tempted Mary to turn Jesus into a little Joseph. Perhaps Mary saw any unique features in Jesus as indicators of how great and wonderful He would become.

There were times when she must have felt like breaking with frustration. What about the time Joseph and Mary lost Jesus? Even though their intellect told them they would find Him safe, their emotions ran wild as they imagined all the things that might have happened to Him. Backtracking, they went to Jerusalem, looking for the slightest clue along the way. Finally they arrived back at the Temple, their last hope. Seeing Jesus, they erupted in exasperation, "Where have you been?" Jesus revealed His growing independence with His reply, "Did you not know that I must be about the vocation I will enter some day?" (Luke 2:48-49, Author). Jesus' statement was not curt or abrasive. It was the response of one who was becoming His own person.

Surely Mary thought about Jesus' statement, wondering exactly what it meant and when this would happen. The years went by and all Mary saw was Jesus standing ankle-deep in shavings. She must have been eager for the beginning of His mission. Maybe, once His mission was underway, there would be those who would understand the things she thought about so deeply. Mary was so eager for Jesus' mission to begin that, at the wedding feast in Cana of Galilee, she wanted Him to use His gifts to overcome the shortsighted thinking of the host and provide more wine. She must have been bewildered when Jesus responded, "O woman, what have you to do with me? My hour has not yet come" (John 2:4).

Mary so wanted Jesus' mission to set things right. After all, being favored by God had not been so favored up to this point. She must have been plunged into despair at Capernaum. Jesus seemed to be living contrary to the religious laws. He seemed to be moving in contradistinction to everything Mary had ever expected of the Messiah. His mission seemed to be going in a direction potently opposite of all she had hoped. So in despair was Mary that she joined Jesus' brothers in the conclusion that her precious Messiah had slipped a cog. They decided to remove Him, by force if necessary, from this erratic ministry (Mark 3:20 ff.). Jesus was told that His mother and brothers were present. How did He respond? With a question, "Who is my mother, and who are my brothers? Here are my mother and my brothers! For whoever does the will of my Father in heaven is my brother, and sister, and mother" (Matt. 12:48-50).

In less than three years, Mary saw the utter collapse of the mission which never began to take the shape she had anticipated. She stood at the foot of the cross, dazed into stark numbness. Only John's Gospel tells of Mary's presence at the cross. She saw the mission, such as it was, and what did she get out of it? John tells us that all she got out of the mission was to be a guest in John's home. "He said to his mother, 'Woman, behold your son!' " And to that disciple He said, "Behold your mother!" (John. 19:26-27). From that hour on, the disciple took her into his own home.

Mary's life did not turn out as she expected. It just isn't in the order of things that a mother outlives her son. Even if Mary were convinced that Jesus had done some strange things, she knew He had done nothing to deserve death, certainly not a death like this. From that hour, that disciple, the only disciple who was at the cross, took Mary as his own mother. But that was small comfort. Consider what she lost: in reality, a son; in her dream, a Messiah who never developed as she expected. She became a hanger-on in somebody else's house. She had a place to lay her head, more than her son ever had. She was the object of the charitable love and care of one who loved Jesus, but she had expected to be the queen of the world.

Mary has come to have a very special place in Christendom. Years later, in the postresurrection church, Mary became free to tell Luke all the things she had kept locked up inside. It took a very special woman to mother the Messiah. This fact alone has given her special significance.

I marvel at Jesus' consciousness and sensitivity in seeking Mary's welfare. While He was dying Jesus was serene and calm enough to think, pray, and plan for others. I can understand how Jesus would be aware of the crowd, buzzing with anticipation and shouting insults. What is troubling is that Jesus prayed, "Father, forgive them." It makes sense that Jesus would be aware of the criminals because they were beside Him. They were in this together, although for different reasons; but nonetheless, they were experiencing the same kind of death. The sensitivity of Jesus is demonstrated in His loving response to one of the criminals, "Today you will be with Me." I am amazed that Jesus could focus on anyone in the middle of this drama. Surely He was in a blind haze. Was He not tempted to think only of Himself and feel only His pain? Yet, He saw his mother, and the fact that He saw her is like a precious kiss. The only kind of kiss He could give her was to see her. It seems like such a small incident, but how much of human life passes in little incidents! How many of us would have avoided such an interaction because of our fear of the pain we might feel?

Epictetus was a Stoic philosopher in the first century. He is the great source of much that is good in ancient Stoicism. He had a wish for his dying:

> I should like best that dying should find me busy at something noble and beneficent and for the good of mankind. But, since that is little likely to befall me, I should choose next to go out, rendering what is due to every relation in life.[7]

Christ, in His dying, lived out both of these aspirations. He died rendering what is due to every primal relation in life, and at the same time accomplishing that which was for the good of all. Jesus died as He lived. How much closer to being human can one get?

Some have concerned themselves with His address, "Woman," having perceived it as curt, cold, and impersonal. The term could be infinitely tender. Jesus had addressed His mother in the same manner at the wedding feast in Cana. Jesus used this term, *gunē,* to redefine the relationship of mother and son. This relational dynamic generally happens in family life as children grow up. As the children begin to see themselves as separate persons from their parents, *daddy* becomes *dad* and *mommy* becomes *mom.* Jesus' use of *gunē* (woman) rather than *mētēr* (mother) demonstrated that she could no longer exercise maternal authority over Him.

We are up close to the cross and we feel uncomfortable. So did the disciples. Only John was willing to be in sight and sound of the cross. There He adopted Mary as His mother. You may have noticed that no questions were asked. It is the nature of the bond of friends, of master and disciple, to bear one another's burdens. Thus, Jesus could say confidently and unashamedly to John, "Behold, your mother."

As we come closer to the cross, as we see how this One died like He lived, the words of A.J. Gossip are an inspiration. With respect to his own death Gossip said,

> God grant that when the dark is falling round us in that last scene of all, when the poorest of us, for once, hold the center of the stage,

may we face death with a like unselfishness—not fidgeting about ourselves, not hurriedly making last-minute preparations, but packed and
ready and waiting for the tide, may we be able eagerly to enter into the
happiness and interest of those around us . . . that for us, too, death
may be no squalid thing, but big and . . . invincible.[8]

The whole world watched and watches Jesus die. No person ever
died in the presence of so many watchers. He died for, and in view
of the whole world; and yet, in the moment of His dying for the whole
world, He reached out to identify with the primal human relationship.
We have watched Him all along His journey, but nowhere was He
more human than when He said, "Behold, your mother." And nowhere in the journey was He more completely worthy, from the
human side, of being called the Son of God.

I Thirst:
John 19:28

We have thought after pushing the lawn mower or after waking up
from surgery with "cotton mouth," that we were thirsty. We have
watched movie scenes of those stranded in the desert and have imagined what real thirst is like. But few if any of us have had the parched
lips and dusty throat that accompany severe dehydration.

We have in this word of Christ, *dipsō,* no postoperative thirst, no
playacting from a desert scene. Here is a real human being who had
all of life wrung out of Him. Through the agonizing experience of
crucifixion He tended to the needs of the crowd, "Father, forgive
them," to the needs of a common thief, "Today you will be with Me,"
and to the needs of His mother, "Behold, your son."

Jesus' reason for saying He was thirsty according to John was to
fulfill Scripture. A portion of Psalm 69 is what Christ quoted. No
doubt Jesus and John were familiar with this psalm, written as personal and community expression by people worshiping God. Jesus and
others read His situation in life and quoted these words as a means
of expressing what was occurring. We often quote Tennyson, Shake-
speare, and others to illustrate and communicate our feelings and
experiences. It was natural for the earlier followers of Christ to find
in their hymnal, the Psalms, words that Jesus Himself had quoted and
that they used to describe their Master.

We have done for ourselves what Jesus did. Who of us has not found a portion of one of the Psalms that described our situation? When such a discovery is made, that passage becomes implanted in our lives. Perhaps in Jesus' cry, "I thirst," He was quoting, as He was when He said, "My God, My God. . . ." Jesus was thirsty, and even this basic need was a temptation to Him. The battle inside was between underexpression and overexpression. Was He tempted to deny His thirst with the claim, "Real men don't get thirsty?" Was He tempted to make a scene and draw the attention of all people to Himself by shouting out how terrible His thirst was? Once again, He walked the straight and narrow path, admitting He was a human being with a basic human need—"I thirst." Whether or not He was quoting, there seems to be a double identifying here. He is identifying with the thirst of all Israel and with a basic human need. All Israel thirsted for, longed for, the Messiah, God's Deliverer. As Moses had brought the children of Israel out of the parched land of Egypt, every Israelite hoped that the Messiah would come to the dry and thirsty land of Israel and bring a spring of living water that never would run dry.

With His cry, "I thirst," Jesus expressed a basic human need. Water is our most basic biological need. Most of us could do without food much longer than we would ever attempt. But without water, a person might exist three days. Isn't it amazing how just a small drink can soothe and comfort? As surgical patients begin to return from the land of the unconscious, a few ice chips can bring great refreshment and comfort, even if only briefly. When a person is near death, about the last thing he can be is thirsty. Perhaps about the last power one has is to drink.

The theme of thirst is a thread which runs throughout the ministry of Christ. "Blessed are those who hunger and thirst for righteousness, for they shall be satisfied" (Matt. 5:6). One of the early events in His ministry was Jesus' encounter with a Samaritan woman at a well in Sychar. In essence, Jesus said to her, "I'm thirsty." His words were, "Give me a drink [of water]" (John 4:7). The conversation expanded from that point and Jesus spoke about an eternal, thirst-quenching source of living water. Jesus claimed to offer that kind of refreshing water which would become a spring of life-giving water within the person. Jesus, who was thirsty, asked for a drink. Then He promised a gift by which one would never be thirsty again. Yet, as His life ended, nearly His last word was, "I thirst." Only John had Jesus saying, "I thirst." Matthew and Mark recorded that gall, a type of pain killer mixed with wine, was offered Jesus when His agony seemed most intense and was expressed in the words, "My God, My God."

Luke interpreted the offering of a mixture of gall and cheap wine to Jesus to have been a means of taunting used by the soldiers. Such an interpretation is uncharacteristic of Luke, who often demonstrated the positive aspects of the outsiders, the Gentiles. If we are to take all four Gospels in order to paint the passion picture of Christ, then there were two drinks offered Christ.

It is John who recorded the need of Christ for a drink and that Jesus drank the wine, a cheap wine such as was a common drink of Roman soldiers. This saying of Christ, "I thirst," is another difficult word for the church. The earlier Gospels don't have it. It has been and continues to be very difficult for people to have a thirsty Messiah. For Him to be thirsty makes Him too human, more human than many are willing to permit. But this is identification with us. Here, on the cross, the Messiah has run to the end of this human track. He has come all the way. With a taste of wine to wet His thirst, He came to the end of human ability and resources and He stood completely identified with us. From John's perspective, Jesus' ministry opened and closed with the same words, "I'm thirsty."

Can you imagine what this word, *dipsō,* "I thirst," must have done to Mary? This may have been the worst cry of all to bear. To hear one of my children cry out in the darkness, "I'm thirsty," and to be unable to give him a cup of water would be horrid. This must have been the worst word for Mary, to hear her son cry out in the midnight of His life, "I'm thirsty." Much earlier Jesus had said that whoever gave a cup of cold water to anyone in His name served the Kingdom. Do you suppose that Jesus had any way of knowing that someday a lad, or a Roman soldier, or a young Jew would run and get something for Him to wet his thirst? Someone unnamed—unknown—soaked a sponge in wine and lifted it to Jesus' lips, and He drank.

Jesus made a sacrament out of every glass of water. He makes a priest out of every stumbling, faltering, fumbling person who moves from a faucet to the person who says, "I'm thirsty." We need to remember what it is to thirst. Every time we take a drink of water, we ought to remember the sacrament of thirst.

Great moments and opportunities come like all other moments and opportunities, and the greatness comes in how we handle the events of the moment. From the teaching of Jesus we can conclude correctly that this "whoever" who lifted a wine-soaked sponge to Jesus' lips was kind to Christ. When Jesus was in the process of dying, this unknown person did something to help Christ through the parched land. There is no need for envy and wishing we could do something as worthwhile just once in our lives. All of us have the same opportunities. Christ always was touched with the feeling of His people's needs and infirmities, and thus He accounted anything done to aid the most insignificant as done to Him.

Jesus died as He lived, caring for the needs of people. He was able to minister to others, even in His dying, because all along He had been sensitive to His personal needs and shared them with the Father. He had spent His life, given it freely, and all of life was wrung out of Him. The last thing He could be was to be thirsty, and the last thing He could do was drink. Jesus said, "I [am] thirsty," so a sponge was soaked in wine, put on a stalk of hyssop, and lifted to His lips. Jesus drank the wine.

My God, Why Have You Forsaken Me?

There are no easy last words. The last words of Christ are difficult, but perhaps none are as difficult as, "My God, why hast thou forsaken Me?" (Matt. 27:46). What is He saying? What does He mean? How are we to understand it? As we examine this word of Christ, we will discover it examining us before we are finished with it.

Was Jesus tempted to curse God and die? He expected the enterprise of being God in the flesh to be filled with risks and difficulties, but did He know it would come to this? The pain was more intense than He had anticipated. The verbal and physical spit were degrading. How could God have gotten Jesus into this? "My God, why [have you] forsaken Me?" may be the ultimate last word of Jesus. As we approach this last word, we are confronted with the three "D's" of traditional interpretation: delirium, desolation, and dereliction.

Was Jesus delirious? Why else would He say, "My God, My God, why [have you] forsaken Me?" Every person has a pain tolerance level. A person may not be able to measure his pain tolerance, but once he has reached a level of pain that he no longer can bear, he may become delirious. Perhaps you have reached the land of delirium at some time in your life. You have, at least momentarily, entered another world. No one can reach you there. Have you ever tried to communicate with one who is delirious? There is no reaching him, even though you are in sight and sound of him and can reach out and touch him. Had the pain become so intense for Jesus that any consciousness was purely and completely self-consciousness? Was He aware, but only aware of Himself?

The twenty-second Psalm is a picture of one who feels forsaken and beleagured but who has unshaken confidence in the glimmer that remained of the presence of God in his consciousness. In the land of delirium beyond Jesus' pain tolerance level, had all memory and hope and otherness been wrung out of Him? Is there anyone among us who, suffering unbounded pain, suspended between heaven and earth on two pieces of wood, could be aware of anything or anyone beyond ourselves? This is delirium. Perhaps Christ was delirious. If so, it happened suddenly. Moments earlier, He had conversed with the common criminals, cared for His mother, and then asked for a drink. Maybe, suddenly, He crossed over into the land of delirium.

Obviously, Jesus was feeling desolate, abandoned. I do not know exactly what such a feeling would be like. I have talked with a few adults who were abandoned as children, and I have sensed the panicky feeling they still experience as they tell about being left and feeling that their existence made no difference to anyone. Their relationships with their parents had counted for nothing. You may have experienced a degree of abandonment or desolation through divorce or the death of a parent, spouse, child, or close friend. I have sensed the ache and hurt that such events have caused in the lives of other people, but I cannot say that I understand, because I have not experienced desolation even to this degree. But many of you have, and can identify more than I with the feeling of desolation that Christ may have experienced.

To feel there is no one with you is desolation. To be abandoned is to be suspended, to belong nowhere, to hang between heaven and earth.

This is what it means to be nailed, abandoned. This is that aloneness where one is under the knife with no prospect of being anywhere else. There is no elsewhere! This is crucifixion: to be tearing apart where one is, with no prospect of movement left, without any Other.[9] The feeling of having been abandoned hangs heavy in this word of Christ, "Why have you forsaken Me?"

But there is more. Is this word a cry of dereliction from Christ?

Dereliction is a strong word. It is the state of being abandoned as worthless. A derelict ship is deserted by both people and the rats, being driven helplessly before the gale. Did Christ fling His agonized "why" against what seemed an uncomprehending sky?

Would God abandon His own Son? Why? Jesus earlier had promised He would never abandon His followers. For what reason would God abandon His Son? Would not such abandonment say there may come some tough times in our lives when God cannot stay with us? There had been other cries to God from this same area of agony. Only a few hours earlier Jesus had said, "Father, if it be possible, let this cup pass from me" (Matt 26:39). From the cross He had prayed, "Father, forgive them." In another moment we will hear Christ pray, "Father, into thy hands I commend my spirit" (Luke 23:46, KJV) God heard the first prayer. He heard the other prayers. Later, He heard the cry, "It is finished" (John 19:30).

These cries do not suggest delirium, desolation, or dereliction. Quite the contrary, prayers such as these demonstrate a most intimate goodness of God and His ultimate dominion over all nations. Many believe that God abandoned Christ and that this word of His depicts the depth of Christ's despair. Martin Dibelius, a New Testament scholar, offers another point of view by saying that you do not quote Scripture in prayer when you have given up your faith. George Buttrick said in a sermon that there hangs in a chapel in Milan an early Renaissance painting of the crucifixion in which, late in the evening, when the light allows, and when viewed from a certain angle, a shadowy figure seems to have been interposed between Christ and the wood of the cross. The artist was trying to say the Father was there, too.

Maybe this cry, "My God, My God," was not—is not—addressed to God. It certainly does not have the warmth of "Dad" that Jesus' other prayers had. What if Christ was talking to His disciples? "My God, My God," captures the agonizing hurt that Christ felt by being abandoned, not by God, but by His disciples. Mark wrote that Jesus called disciples for two reasons: first, they were to be with Him— friends, companions; and second, they were to proclaim the good news. Jesus invited people to be His disciples, to be with Him. The intent of the invitation was that they would be with Christ, come what may. But the cross came, and where were the disciples? Shattered.

scared, and scattered! John was the only one of the twelve who dared show His face.

The others were hiding, crying out in their souls, "Is it I?" Abandonment is betrayal by proxy. It may be more subtle than Judas' approach, but it is just as cold and destructive, and cuts as deeply. Hear the agony of Christ, "My God, My God, why [have you] forsaken Me?" When Christ needed companionship and friendship most desperately, His friends were not there.

The last word also addresses us. We have promised to be followers, disciples of Christ. We have taken His identity into our lives by calling ourselves Christians. Our promise has exceeded our practice. We too have denied and betrayed Christ. Whenever we have sinned we have abandoned Him and as the author of Hebrews suggests we crucify the Son of God on our own account and hold Him up to contempt (Heb. 6:6). Jesus' last word, "My God, My God, why have you forsaken Me?" also is spoken to each of us.

Jesus died as He lived. Ernst Kasemann insists that this cry be understood as evidence of this. Jesus died with God's word on His lips and with unshaken trust in Him who alone and always is one's true help. If God turned His back on Jesus, we are saying that there are some difficult times when we might expect God to check out on us if life becomes too strenuous. This makes faith in God rather precarious, causing us to wonder if our present situation is the one when God will pull out His support. The promise of God is that He always will be with us. That was a promise by which Jesus lived and died. Jesus lived out a life the way a life is to be lived. He invites us to do the same. The source of help and hope to live as Jesus did is God who never abandons a person solely to his own resources.

Jesus, feeling the loneliness and abandonment of His companions, tells us what it is like to be utterly human, left solely to our own resources. Jesus' words, "My God, My God," are an expression of loneliness and perplexity over the betrayal, the desertion, and the cross. As much as is possible for God to dwell in a human being, God dwelt in Christ. In essence, the Jewish leaders, the Roman soldiers, and the crowd had God in their hands. The cross displays what people do when they have God in their hands.

Matthew and Mark were the only New Testament writers who recorded this abandonment word of Christ from the cross. It is the only last word they recorded. The other six last words are found in

Luke and/or John. *Abandonment* was and is a difficult word for the church. Some thought Jesus was calling for Elijah. According to the Old Testament, Elijah transcended death, and legend had it that he came to the aid of persons in great distress. I do not know if any true Jew could have heard Jesus say "Eloi" and mistaken it for "Elijah." People can hear almost anything they wish to hear. Those who heard His cry knew Him. Those who had no wish to hear, those who had no hope of hearing, heard Him call Elijah, and ran to substitute vinegar. They offered Him a type of cheap wine similar to vinegar, probably in an attempt to deaden the pain, because they thought He was delirious from physical pain. But the emotional pain of abandonment by friends cannot be lessened with painkillers. Jesus knew that, and His words verbalized the deep agony He felt because of the desertion of those in whom He had invested so much of Himself.

As Jesus looked in disbelief into the absence of His friends, He was tempted to say nothing. At this late hour, what good would His words be? Three years of talking had brought Him to a cross where His friends would not show their faces. Jesus may have been tempted to say too much, to lash out in verbal abuse at His absent supporters. Rather, He chose a third alternative. He simply called out to His absent friends to give an account of themselves. Why had they abandoned Him? This is a last word that resisted the shortcuts of saying nothing or saying too much, and it penetrated to the essence of His disciples' actions. What a confrontational last word this is!

Jesus is suspended between heaven and earth on two pieces of wood. To whom is He looking when in anguish He utters, "My God, My God, why [have you] forsaken Me?" I submit He is looking at the crowd, at us. We are scared and scattered, hiding, seeking asylum somewhere, anywhere. Cutting through the darkness of noonday is this stark cry, this last word spoken to us, "My God, My God, why have you, and you, and you, forsaken Me?"

It Is Finished:
John 19:30

There is so little in life that is ever finished. We touch the high spots hurriedly. The sand in the hourglass runs out. We must stop. The ball game may be over. The exam may have been taken. The funeral service may have been conducted. We may summarize by saying, "It is past." But who of us can say that anything is ever finished? I do not know the filing system you use to keep up with pertinent information in your life. I have a hunch that somewhere in your system there is a file labeled, "Unfinished business," and it is chock full. Whenever you dare look in it, you take only a brief glance, are overwhelmed, and conclude, "I'll never finish any of this." We may work briefly on unfinished business, become exasperated, and quit.

Having listened to the taunts of the crowd and feeling the abandonment of friends, was Jesus tempted to conclude His life had been wasted energy? Did He now want to resign from life and get it over? Even at the very end of life, Jesus spoke a word that expressed His resistance to giving in to the easy, quick solution.

The Gospels report differently the last breath of Jesus. Matthew and Mark said that He gave a loud cry and died. Luke reported that He cried out in a loud voice, "Father! In your hands I place my spirit!" (Luke 23:46, GNB) and died. John wrote that Jesus said, "It is finished," bowed His head, and died (19:30). The Gospel writers had different eyewitnesses to this tragedy. Matthew and Mark's witnesses were watching from a distance. They only heard Him say, "My God, My God." The reporters to Luke and John heard Jesus say much more. The last of the last words of Christ reverberated against the stark silence of those who watched. What do they say to us who stand uncomfortably, first on one foot and then the other, and watch? Jesus did not die by some decree of God's will to buy off Satan. He did not die to satisfy a pagan god of legal righteousness, or to ransom a kidnapped person, or to keep us from having to die. Here Christ, by an act of faith, turned the outcome over to God. It is not as if the Son of God went His whole life without calling on God and then called on God when time was gone. It is not as if God had never before heard His voice. Here is the last picture of an unshaken faith agonizing its way to breathe its last, when the final surge of pain is over, with the sure and restful sigh of a tired child He prayed, "Father, I place My care in Your hands" (Author).

John records a different word as the last word of Christ. *Tetelestai,* "It is finished." Jesus said, "It is finished," and died. Hope was gone, or so it seemed. Everything for which He had toiled and sacrificed seemed gone, lost, and soon to be forgotten. Maybe Calvary did mean that Jesus and His kind always would be so wide of the mark, so absolutely beside the point that they were bound to come out all through the ages at the little end of everything and be wiped clean off the slate at last. After all, nothing had come of all that Jesus had taught, planned, done, and suffered, except for a little group who claimed to love and a scattered group who had believed in Him and fled.

Luke's account of the last words of Christ opens and closes with the same address, "Father." Luke began with "Father, forgive them," and concluded with, "Father, into your hands. . . ." The intimate, loving relationship with God as Father which began early in Jesus' life, which nurtured Him in His growth, His struggles, and His living, also sustained Him in His dying. Here we are only three hours later in the life of Christ than when we began this chapter. But with what intensity Christ lived those three hours! Once again, with Christ being supremely human, He experienced the truth of another's words as expressive of His confidence. "Father, into Your hands . . ." is a quote from Psalm 31.

This prayer by Christ reveals an unashamed commitment of trust fully discharged. There may not be many who are conscious of any sense of completion when death comes to them. Jesus knew and accepted all along that He was mortal, that He would die. Even so, there was every reason for Jesus to have had a sense of incompletion. He was cut off at the threshold of life. No accusation could be supported against Him. He was kind. The most pathetic commentary on human life is the list of His enemies. Here we see Him coming to an untimely death just as He is turning into manhood, his ministry just budding, barely in the spring of its development. The possibilities were unfathomed and the hopes were unrealized. Wherever He had gone around the countryside, trouble had followed. Jesus could not even die in a solitary state, for two thieves were crucified with Him. The ones he had attempted to teach had betrayed, denied, and fled. Those who were closest to Him in living were at a distance in His dying, saying, "We never thought it would come to this." Even with all of this, Jesus could pray, "Father! Into Your hands. . . ."

This prayer of Christ was not sad resignation, as the medieval artists tended to portray. Although the biblical accounts tell that He stumbled as He walked toward Golgotha, there is no indication anywhere that there was any stumbling caused by uncertainty. Actually, the opposite seems evident. The whole day with all its tragedy, horror, and awfulness seems pervaded by a sense of untroubled certainty.

There are numerous examples of uncertainty, but not in Christ.

There was no certainty in Pilate. He came in, went out, sat down, stood up, gave judgments, went back on them, excused himself by allowing others to decide for him, and washed his hands. There was no certainty in the frantic mob. Their vacillation is depicted in their cheers—"Hosanna!" one day and "Crucify!" the next. There was no certainty in the frightened disciples. Peter spoke with the greatest commitment and acted with the least. The disciples observed the crucifixion from a distance. The Sanhedrin expressed no certainty. They were disorganized and confused. Some members, but not all, were certain that if they could be rid of Jesus, their troubles would end.

Only Jesus seemed deliberate, masterful, certain. Each step He chose. He refused the drug. The accusers, the crowd, and the executioners were forgiven. A thief was made the object of a royal promise. A sorrowing mother was given over to the tender hands of a disciple. With a little wine to wet His thirst, He prayed, "Father. . . ."

Following twenty-four hours of agony, taunting misery, trial, and crucifixion, Jesus said, "It is finished." But His statement was not about twenty-four hours of life, it was about thirty-three years of living. How life is to be lived was lived out by Him. As a human being He could lay out a life as God intended a life to be laid out. He could finish.

In contrast, John Ruskin's comments about art are descriptive of our attempts at finishing:

> Our best finishing is but coarse and blundering work after all. We may smooth and soften and sharpen till we are sick at heart; but take a good magnifying glass to our miracle of skill, and the invisible edge is a jagged saw, and the silky thread a rugged cable and the soft surface a granite desert. . . . God alone can finish; and the more intelligent the human mind becomes, the more infiniteness of interval is felt between human and divine work in this respect.[10]

What can the best of us take back to God? Some broken promises? A few attempts that came to little? Maybe some dreams that died, or that came true and proved most disappointing? We all use our brief spans of life learning how to live; and, having learned a little, get no chance to put it into practice. We often conclude that because a segment of life has ended that we have done our best. That is relief.

Jesus expressed certainty in knowing that He had carried through completely and His work was finished.

But what was finished? Christ enabled people to know God and to know humanity and life as they are created by God to be. Jesus Christ is the first human being. He is the true Person, the Head of the race. The state of Kentucky is known for thoroughbred race horses. A thoroughbred is a beautiful creature, sleek, fast, competitive. I could use numerous words to describe a thoroughbred, but if you really want to know what one is like, the best thing I could do would be to take you to a horse farm in Paris, Kentucky, and show you Triple Crown winner Secretariat. He represents the best of the breed. If you want to know what a human being should be like, the best thing I can do is to show you Jesus Christ. He is the best of the breed.

Wasn't the temptation there for Jesus to beg for more time, another minute, another hour? Having taken the long way around all along, perhaps it was not so difficult to do the same here. He examined the life that He had laid out. He had finished. That is a last word for us because we are so far away from finishing anything, especially laying out our lives like God intended lives to be lived. Jesus identified with humanity, with us. As death came upon Him, Jesus turned up an empty cup. Death took nothing from Jesus Christ because He had poured out all the contents of life. He is now with us, for us, and in us.

Each Gospel writer attempted to record the drama of Christ identifying with humanity. Apparently, Matthew and Mark had the same source of information about the final moment in Jesus' life. "He gave a loud cry and died" (Matt. 27:50; Mark 15:37, Author). Luke and John apparently had sources different from each other and different from Matthew and Mark. Luke reported that Jesus' experience on the cross closed as it opened, with a prayer. "Father. . . . !" John depicted a strong expression of finality, "It is finished." To be identified with us is to be dying, to be dead. The dead Jesus left everything in the Father's hands.

Several others tried to do something. Joseph of Arimathea went to Pilate and asked for the body of the rabbi. Pilate said, "If it is dead, take it away. We are finished with it" (John 19:38-39, Author). Nicodemus also helped Joseph with Jesus' body. The women wanted to scent the body, wrap it, and care tenderly for it. Nevertheless, all that was left was a dead body that once had housed the living voice that said, "Father, forgive them," "Today you will be with Me," "Behold your mother," "My God, My God," "I thirst," "Father, into Your hands."

The rest belonged to God.

Notes

1. Henry Turlington, *The Broadman Bible Commentary* (Nashville: Broadman Press, 1969), vol. 8, p. 387.

2. Gottob Schrenk, "Pater," Gerhard Kittel and Gerhard Friedrich, eds. (*Theological Dictionary of the New Testament* (Grand Rapids: William B. Eerdmans Publishing Co.), vol. 5, p. 984.

3. Aland, Kurt, et. als., eds. *The Greek New Testament,* (London: United Bible Societies, 1966), p. 311. (Omitted in Papyrus 75, Codex Vaticanus, Codex Bezae, and others)

4. Carlyle Marney, *He Became Like Us* (Nashville: Abingdon Press, 1964), p. 18.

5. Joachim Jeremias," "Paradeisos, " Gerhard Kittel and Gerhard Friedrich, eds., *Theological Dictionary of the New Testament* (Grand Rapids: William B. Eerdmans Publishing Company), vol. V, p. 765.

6. Charles F. Pfeiffer, *Baker's Bible Atlas,* (Grand Rapids: Baker Book House, 1961), p. 124.

7. Pfeiffer, p. 41.

8. Ibid, p. 41.

9. Ibid, p. 41.

10. *The Interpreter's Bible,* (Nashville: Abingdon Press, 1957), Vol. 8., n.p.n.

6

The Lasting Words of Jesus

John 11:1-27; 16:25-33

Many of the words of Jesus have lasted twenty centuries after close scrutiny and serious examination. Jesus' words have been both timely and timeless, ringing true in lives across the centuries. In this closing chapter I want to focus on Jesus' parabolic living, discuss two lasting words of Jesus, and highlight three afterwords Jesus spoke to His disciples.

Parabolic Living

Salvation is the central concern of biblical religion as with all religions. In biblical religion, salvation means coming to one's senses and experiencing the love of God that is continually being offered.

As the Gospel writers explained it, salvation is a new kind of existence in Christ. Salvation resides in the nature of God Himself rather than in an external event of any kind. A variety of images were used by the New Testament writers to aid people in developing a picture of the salvation that Christ offered. The teaching about salvation is known as the doctrine of atonement. As first one facet and then another of Jesus' life has been emphasized, at least eight theories of atonement have developed. There are adherents for each of these theories who will insist that, to be a member of the faith community of Christ, one must claim belief in one specific atonement theory to the exclusion of the others.

The word *atonement* appears only once in the King James Version of the New Testament (Rom. 5:11). In this passage *katallagēn* is translated *atonement* but everywhere else in the New Testament the same word is translated *reconciliation.* The word *atonement* means *at-one-ment:* a person and God united.

The New Testament writers were overwhelmed by the majesty and mystery of a God who loved the world so deeply that He took unbelievable and indescribable measures to communicate this love. Attempting to relate through the written Word the activity of the living Word of God, these writers grasped for illustrations to express the love of God in understandable analogies. As a result New Testament authors suggested that God's reconciling activity in Jesus Christ was like purchasing a slave's freedom (1 Tim. 2:5-6), or like giving up one's life in order to benefit others' lives (John 15:13), or like sacrificing a human life as animals had been sacrificed in the past (Heb. 10:1-18), or like performing a service for or acting in the place of others (Rom. 3:21-26), or like giving satisfaction to God for humanity's sin (Eph. 1:7-10).

The Gospels tell the story of Jesus seeking to save people. He is depicted as forgiving sins on the simple basis of a person's willingness to receive the forgiveness. Jesus was put to death while He was engaging in saving people, not so they might be saved later. Saving sinners is grounded in who God eternally is, not a transaction required to open God to the possibility of saving people. What we see in Christ is an extension, intensification, and personification of what God always has been doing. The reconciling work of God is mysterious but always it is at God's initiative. Change is evoked in people, not in God.

In this sense the cross of Christ has existed from the foundation and formation of the world. Certainly the cross was a particular event at Golgotha, but it also was part of the eternal nature of God. When God created the world He gave humanity freedom. In giving humankind freedom God gave freedom and power to people. That made it possible for people to choose freely to worship and serve Him, to place their trust and love in God. Having such freedom also made it possible for people to reject God, to distrust and hate Him. Thus the cross was in the nature of God from the beginning of creation. When the Word became flesh, the Word was open to understanding and misunderstanding. Salvation or redemption is in who Christ is, not in what was done to Him.

Jesus spoke and lived parabolically. His encounter with Zacchaeus is a living parable that succinctly portrays Jesus' purpose in His ministry which He summarized at the end of that event. "Today salvation has come to this house, since he also is a son of Abraham. For the Son of man came to seek and to save the lost" (Luke 19:9-10). Jesus embodied the essence of the cross when He associated and ate with publicans and sinners. When Jesus invited Himself to Zacchaeus' house for lunch, the religious community was offended. He so contradicted the religious values of the town by His action that the people rejected Him.

Salvation comes to all people like it came to Zacchaeus. It comes from the unchanging nature of God and is possible whenever a person by faith opens Himself to the presence of God. Jesus Christ is the eternal God saving sinners when and where they open their lives to Him.

Two Lasting Words of Jesus

Whenever and wherever people close their lives to God, reject the love and grace that God offers, then they crucify Christ afresh (Heb. 6:6). Much of what makes Good Friday and Easter so traumatic is what they say about people and about God. Good Friday tells all the world what people do when they have God in their hands. Good Friday was the darkest, saddest day of God's creation. The carpenter from Nazareth was too good to be safe; thus, He was killed on Golgotha. Crucifixion is what people did and do to Christ.

I Am the Resurrection: John 11:25

When all of history had arrived at dusk and the disciples' lives were engulfed in darkness, the remembered words of Jesus must have sounded like tinkling cymbals signifying nothing. These had been His words of assurance: "I am the resurrection and the life; he who believes in me, though he die; yet shall he live, and whoever believes in me shall never die. Do you believe this?" (John 11:25-26). Jesus had flung out promises and called up hopes that had long been dead, getting them up from unmarked, forgotten graves. But at His crucifixion there was no evidence of resurrection or life. Death was pervasive. Jesus died and was buried, and with Him were buried the hopes and dreams of many who had been grabbed by His promises and halfway believed them, believed them because they wanted to or needed to or had to in order to survive. Now their hopes were in the tomb with the One who had raised their hopes. Good Friday demonstrated what people did when they had God in their hands.

It was after the resurrection of Lazarus and some time before His own that Jesus said, "I am the resurrection and the life." The sign and reality of resurrection are seen in Lazarus and Jesus. The sign of resurrection was shown in Lazarus. As a sign, Lazarus' resurrection

did not directly disclose the reality of the resurrection but only provided an earthly analogy to it in what may more accurately be called
the physical restoration or resuscitation of Lazarus.

A glance at the resurrections of Lazarus and Jesus calls for a second
look at these two events. The second look reveals contrasts in these
two resurrections. Lazarus came forth from his tomb after men had
rolled away the stone. Jesus needed no such human help to move the
stone from His grave. When Lazarus was resurrected, he was still
bound by his grave clothes. Jesus passed through His and left them
behind. Lazarus returned to earthly relationships and died again.
Jesus ascended to God. Lazarus had no more to offer the world after
his resurrection than before except a new lease on life which pointed
away from himself to Jesus as its source. Faith was required to see in
Lazarus more than a medical marvel, to believe that he signified the
possibility of eternal life in the midst of time. Jesus kindled and raised
up such faith.

Lazarus was a sign of resurrection, but Jesus was the reality of
resurrection. Easter demonstrates what God does when He has people
in His hands. Jesus put Himself in God's hands and God raised Him
to a qualitatively new life that no longer knew death. Resurrection is
not a continuation of this life but is the annihilation of death into the
new, eternal life.

There are people who do not need another life. They would be at
a loss to know what to do with it. They have enough difficulty killing
time. It would be an even drearier existence attempting to kill eternity.
It seems to matter little to the person who counts only earthly years
by what he does with himself during those years. However, when a
person is convinced that for the whole family of humankind there is
new, eternal life, then today assumes august importance. One can only
use today scrupulously because of its incalculable connections. Is it
not paradoxical that those who are aware of the most time in life
concern themselves with using the most time wisely?

Everything for which Jesus cared required more time than this life
afforded. It called for an eternity, life beyond death. He spent Himself
giving people an ideal which they could not attain within the span of
earthly days. It was a mockery to set before people any such ideal as
godlikeness unless He could assure them of sufficient time in which
to develop it. With the thief on the cross asking forgiveness, Christ

took it for granted that there was time enough for the penitent bandit to become as perfect as God is perfect.

Jesus was a venturer. He marched into Jerusalem to offer Himself to the city. He knew He was hazarding death, but it seems He always took chances based on the assumption of more life in store in which to continue the venture. He staked everything on laying down His life, believing He would take up His life again.

Through the resurrection of Christ, God said no to the judgment hall, no to Golgotha, no to the tomb, and no to living on the wrong side of Easter. The trial of Christ confirmed the verdict that He was too good to be safe in the hands of people. The trial of Jesus was a mockery of justice. We make a mockery of justice when we see our word as the last word on another's life. We have enough difficulty making sound decisions about ourselves. Why do we think we have the discernment to make decisions for others and about the destiny of their lives? God said no to the judgment hall where they tried Jesus. That was not the final judgment of the Son that God had sent into the world.

God said no to Golgotha where they crucified Jesus. Death is the cruel enemy of life but people often make it an ally in their expediency to deal with matters that are too difficult to handle. People were fearful of the change Christ sought. The only alternative many were willing to consider was to do away with the change Agent. God's no said that crucifixion is not the solution to deal with One who is too good to be safe. The crucifixion was not the last word about the One whom God sent.

To the grave where they buried Jesus, God said no. A tomb is damp and cold, lifeless. The grave is man's response to death. What else can we do when someone dies but bury the dead? There is no other word that human beings can offer, but God is not bound by our finitude. His thoughts are not our thoughts, nor His ways our ways. God said no the grave.

The no of God means that we do not have to settle down in the grim facts of which the cross is the worst of them. To all of us who would live on the other side of Easter, God says no. Is that not much of our difficulty? We attempt to live on the wrong side of Easter. To try to live on the other side of Easter is not to live but to exist. God offers us abundant life rather than mere existence. One of the lasting words of Jesus is, "I am the resurrection and the life; he who believes in me though he die, yet shall he live, and whoever lives and believes in me shall never die" (John 11:25-26). As Paul Scherer said, "God's world, no matter how it looks, is not the kind of place where you can finish off the Sermon on the Mount with a hammer and some nails."[1]

To hear the no of God encourages us to say yes. To say yes to the resurrection of Christ means not only to affirm His resurrection but also to experience our own resurrection. If Good Friday is the saddest, darkest day of creation, symbolizing what we do with God when we have God in our hands, then Easter is the gladdest, brightest day of creation, symbolizing what God does with us when He has us in His hands.

Easter compels us to say yes. It symbolizes a new beginning, another chance. Maybe it is our second chance or our two thousandth. Easter pushes us to say yes because it is a word about life and death. Easter says that God shares with us fully all that it means to be human, even the deepest tragedies of our lives. In part Easter is the church's way of saying that God refuses to stop loving people like you and me just because our bodies die. We matter ultimately to God. Just as God created us in His image and shared passionately and fully our human condition, suffering with us in the midst of history, thus He continues to value us and to love us infinitely even in death.

God does not carelessly and idly toss aside human life that He has created in His image. Easter says the opposite. God takes creation seriously and what He has called into being out of creative love, what He agonized over in the middle of history also is cared for infinitely, even in the face of death.

Easter is a lasting word for us. It is God's way of saying no to false trials, executions, and graveyards. John Masefield's play, *The Trial of Jesus,* expresses poignantly why resurrection is a lasting word.

In the play Pilate's wife asked the centurion if he thought Jesus was really dead. Upon indicating that he did not, she asked him where he thought He was. The centurion indicated that he thought Jesus was out in the world in such a way that no one could stop His truth.

Easter confirms a lasting word from Jesus, "I am the resurrection and the life; he who believes in me, though he die, yet shall he live, and whoever lives and believes in me shall never die" (John 11:25-26).

I Have Overcome the World: John 16:33

People have been obsessed with the words of Christ. Immeasurable time and energy have been invested in discovering what Jesus said. The red letter edition of the New Testament was developed to highlight Jesus' words. Recently my eight-year-old daughter asked to look at my Bible. After thumbing through the pages for a few minutes she commented, "Jesus didn't say anything in your Bible." It was not a red letter edition. Even in the red letter edition of the New Testament we do not have all that Jesus said. Surely during three years of ministry He said more of value and instruction than is recorded in the Gospels. Even collecting all of the recorded sayings of Jesus from the four Gospels, many of which are duplicates, does not form a lengthy treatise. Actually, about all we have are the illustrations because about all that remained embedded in the hearers' minds that Matthew, Mark, Luke, and John recorded were the stories Jesus told. If anything is remembered from a book or a sermon, is it not a story, a bit of humor, or an illustration? This was true of Christ. Take away the parables that He spoke and lived and a blank would be left, like the gaps on the walls of the British galleries in World War II when the masterpieces were taken down and hidden.

Jesus told His disciples that He had used figures and illustrations to communicate with them (John 16:25) but there would be a time when He would speak plainly to them. Jesus' intent had not been to conceal insight from His followers but what He said required careful thought for the meaning to take root. Jesus was suggesting that a change would occur in the disciples caused by their increased insight and understanding.

The disciples' immediate response was that now they were understanding. They, like Professor Higgins in *My Fair Lady* were saying, "By George, I think we've got it." But how could the disciples be so blind for so long and then see this clearly so quickly? Has it not happened to all of us? Some new insight comes to us and the light goes on in the darkness of our minds. Suddenly some things make sense and fit together that previously never seemed to go together. The insight had been there all along. The only newness in it was its newness to us.

There is a trap in our newfound insight. Like the early disciples we yield to the temptation to claim the great strides of growth we now will take and the significant improvements we will make in multiple areas of our lives. We celebrate prematurely all the confidence we have that we will be loyal, faithful disciples.

The last basketball game I played in high school was a tournament game against a rival school. We were running our offense well, making a high percentage of our shots, playing aggressive, solid defense. The game was intense. We had the opposition on the ropes. We had doubled the score of our opponent. We were going to win! The buzzer sounded. We all breathed a sigh of relief, but it was only the end of the first quarter. We lost the game.

Jesus' disciples had gained new insight. As a result they made strong, stern promises and assurances to Jesus and to each other. Jesus broke in on their enthusiasm and premature celebrating. He said, "You will be scattered . . . and leave me alone" (John 16:32). It was only the first quarter. This was unthinkable to those first disciples, and it is unthinkable to us. The last week of Christ's life represents betrayal and denial with the spotlight on Judas and Peter. There are other betrayers. We are they and the spotlight is on us, and we are not seen in a very good light.

Jesus said the hour had come when they would all scatter. The hour of scattering happens every year. More people come together to worship on Easter than any other single day of the year. We claim that we gather to celebrate resurrection, but resurrection is a foreign concept to us. Like the first disciples we claim to possess the understanding that faith needs, but our comprehension is shallow because we refuse to experience the cross, the pouring out of our lives, the giving of ourselves, without which we cannot experience resurrection in our daily living.

Public worship is a spectator event for too many of us. We come to worship wanting to receive, but with little if any intention of giving of ourselves. The excitement and enthusiasm of Easter worship may stir the fire in our bones briefly and we go away saying, "It has been good to have been in the house of the Lord." The buzzer sounds. We are relieved. We look up next week, next month, or next year to discover that it is only the first quarter. We have scattered and left Christ alone with our shallow insights and empty promises.

What type of response might we expect from the One we have abandoned? Reprimand? Rejection? A guilt-inducing tirade? Does not one or all of these responses identify how we would respond to any who abandon us? After all, our relationships are based on the condition if a person does not remain a faithful friend during times of stress and duress, then we cast him out of our lives convinced he really never had cared.

When life was crumbling around Him, Jesus remained calm and serene. The secret to His calmness is revealed in the statement, "For the Father is with me" (John 16:32). Jesus' confidence, faith, and hope were in God. We put our confidence in things we can see and feel. Then we are crushed amid the ruins of all that did not stand as we had expected. In contrast, Christ was calm and confident because He and God could face anything together.

Christ had unabashed confidence and trust in His disciples, then and now. He was loyal to those who were disloyal to Him. Jesus stood by His choice of disciples and believed in them. Even when they did not believe in Him or themselves, Christ believed in them. When they were scattered and stood a long way from the cross, Jesus prayed, "Father, forgive them."

No one knew God and people like Jesus knew them. He knew the weaknesses of His disciples. They let Him down and He asked them in the time of His greatest need, "Why have you forsaken me?" Even in this intense aloneness He still loved and trusted them. We claim to forgive persons for their dishonesty or disloyalty to us, vowing never to trust them again. Jesus was able to forgive and trust. He saw people as they were and loved them as they were. When they were disloyal, He was willing to start over with them.

To these who in the twinkling of an eye rose sharply and fell flatly Jesus said, "In the world you have tribulation" (John 16:33a). He made no attempt to conceal the cost or to minimize the dangers of discipleship. To the contrary, He seized every opportunity to point out the cost and dangers of discipleship while simultaneously affirming His confidence in God. A Scottish plowboy-martyr said to a fellow sufferer as the end of life drew ghastly near, "God never guaranteed to keep us out of troubles, but he did promise to bring us through the worst of them. And he will do it."[2]

Jesus said to those He knew would fail Him, "Be of good cheer." He continued loving, forgiving, and trusting others. This One who was falsely arrested, unfairly tried, unjustly condemned, and innocently executed said, "I have overcome the world" (V. 33b). This is a faith that cannot be beaten. Surely this is a Master worth following.

The world did its worst to Jesus. The world's last words for Jesus were "Crucify Him." But those were not the last words and they were not Jesus' last words for the world. When the disciples collected their composure after the death and resurrection of Christ, when the shock and numbness had worn off, when they came to their senses, they discovered that "Crucify Him" were not the last words. The last words and the lasting words of Christ were "be of good cheer, I have overcome the world" (John 16:33b). Jesus' words were confirmed by God's activity. The clearest illustration that Christ overcame the world was His resurrection.

Easter is the single most important day of the year for the Christian. Every Easter, Christians gather and before the day is over they are scattered disciples. They need to be reminded that Easter is the first day and not the last. The lasting words of Christ were spoken for the living of the first day and every day. Christ's lasting words call all followers to resurrected living. Easter is the dawn of life, not the dusk. Easter is the sunrise of many tomorrows rather than the sunset of all of the yesterdays. The lasting words of Christ that pervade this experience are these, "I have overcome the world" (John 16:33 *b*).

Afterwords

The appearances of the risen Christ have prominent importance in the Gospel of John. What Jesus said during these appearances are afterwords that have had lasting meaning and value for His followers.

Go Tell My Brothers: John 20:17

As John tells the story, Mary Magdalene was on her way to Jesus' tomb before daybreak. Maybe she was going to prepare the body more properly for burial because Joseph and Nicodemus had been so rushed on the eve of the sabbath. Perhaps she wanted to visit the place where she last saw Jesus.

Whatever her reasons were for going, when Mary was within sight of the tomb she saw the stone had been removed. She assumed the body was gone. Either those who had killed Jesus had taken the body to dismember it or grave robbers, who were common, had stolen the body. Without checking in the tomb, Mary Magdalene ran to tell Peter and John that "They have taken the Lord out of the tomb" (John 20:2). Peter and John ran to the tomb. John got there first but did not go in. Some suggest that he got there first because he was younger and could run faster. Peter went in and then John entered. The grave clothes were neatly in order. John believed, and then the disciples went back home.

Mary Magdalene apparently was just returning to the tomb when Peter and John were leaving. She was crying. This time she looked into the tomb and saw two messengers, but they were of no help. She wanted and needed to find the body. She turned away from the tomb and there was Jesus, but she did not recognize Him.

Is it so strange that Mary did not recognize Jesus? She was overcome with grief. She never thought life would come to this. The only person who had ever treated Mary as a person was Jesus, and now He was dead. She was in a state of shock and confusion. She was searching here and there, not knowing where to search, but unable not to search.

Mary did not see Jesus because she was searching for a dead Christ. No one can ever find something or someone who does not exist. Many people keep making the same mistake Mary made. They are looking for a Christ who does not exist. The Christ they know lived over nineteen hundred years ago. The record of what He did and taught and suffered moves and impresses them. In thought they often take their stand on Calvary with a very real emotion in their hearts and new inspiration surging up in them. But they have no experience with the risen Lord. Their faith, genuine as it is, is less than Christianity.

A further note is that in all her searching it was not Mary who came upon Christ, but Christ who found Mary. Relationship with God is not a chance development in which, if we are fortunate, we might find what or whom we search for. God is searching for us when we have lost Him and know it, and when we do not even miss Him. God is searching for each of us. He will not lightly let us go. He has missed us and He wants us back with Him again.

Although Mary was searching with her whole being, she did not recognize Christ. So often all that we see is some needy and perhaps unattractive soul; someone who does not appeal to us, but who lacks friendship and claims assistance. "Did you not recognize Me?" asks the Master. "That was I. And inasmuch as you do it to the least of these . . . you do it to Me" (Matt. 25:40, Author). But we, like Mary, suppose Him to be the gardener.

But then Jesus said one word to her. He called her by name, and the way He said "Mary" caused her to know who He was. She had heard Him call her name before and the way He had dealt with her before brought healing. No doubt the way Jesus said, "Mary" flooded her with hope.

There are many details of importance in John's Gospel, of which the experience of Mary Magdalene with the risen Christ is very significant. Each of the Gospel accounts tells of Christ's appearance to a woman or women. Matthew, speaking of the response of the women to the risen Lord, wrote, "And they came up and took hold of his feet, and worshiped him" (Matt. 28:9). Luke said, "But these words seemed to them an idle tale, and they did not believe them" (Luke 24:11). There have been many men who considered what women told them to be idle tales, and vice versa. I wonder if we will ever get beyond filtering what someone tells us, because of that person's sexual identity? Mark and John tell that Christ appeared to Mary Magdalene, but neither made a reference to other women. Mark says the companions of Christ did not believe the testimony of Mary Magdalene.

Is it any wonder that they refused to believe Mary Magdalene? There were numerous reasons not to believe her. First, she was a woman. In the Jewish world of the first century the testimony of a woman was not highly trusted. A woman's testimony certainly was regarded as inferior to that of a man. Second, Mary was from Magdala. Magdala was a notoriously wicked town and there was the prejudiced tendency to discount as untrustworthy most of what any citizen of Magdala had to say. Third, there was a question mark about Mary's sanity. Jesus had cast out seven demons from her. Emotional and mental struggles still prejudice us against persons. We may say of another, "You know he's been seeing a psychiatrist." We make seeing a psychiatrist like the plague and imply that anything a person says who has been in therapy is suspect. Mary Magdalene had seemed improved since she had associated with Jesus, but now apparently she was regressing. She was claiming to have seen and to have talked to One whom the whole community knew was dead. Not only that, she claimed He talked to her. If the followers of Christ could discount and discredit Mary's testimony, maybe she would keep quiet. The thief on the cross was the least likely person to be acceptable to God, according to our standards. Also according to our standards, Mary Magdalene was the least qualified to handle the most momentous news in spiritual history.

The empty tomb was not proof of the resurrection. Someone could have slipped into the cemetery in the night and stolen the body. The proof of the resurrection was the appearance of the risen Lord. His appearances were made to those who had followed Him, had seen Him die, and knew that He had been buried. Can you imagine the shock, excitement, and panic which erupted as Mary began to realize what had taken place? Apparently part of Her response was to cling to Christ. She would not let Him out of her sight again!

As John told it, Jesus said to Mary, "Do not hold me" (John 20:17). The temptation always is just around the corner to keep a relationship the way it used to be. But relationships can never remain static. Relationships involve people who are growing, changing, learning. As people relate to one another, their relationships either deepen or become superficial.

Jesus was saying to Mary that a change had occurred. He wanted her to share in the reality of His resurrection. Mary was being given an inkling of what the resurrection meant, both to Jesus and to His followers. This was an invitation by Jesus for His followers to begin living resurrected lives. It was an invitation to die to living too much for themselves and to rise to live in a new dimension of service to God.

Jesus asked Mary to go tell His brothers whom she had seen. These whom He had called to be learners and servants, these who had failed Him by betraying, denying, and scattering, He called brothers! We all have heard horrid descriptions of the Day of Judgment. I wonder if it will be as alarming as we think. Here there is no word of condemnation or reproach. But stepping across the wide gulf of shame that had opened between Him and them, our Lord began again on the old friendly and trustful terms, even drew nearer to them than ever. He would not lose faith nor affection for those who had failed Him when He most needed them. Christ is not ashamed of us. He is loyal to the most underserving of us as we limp back out of the sad mess we have made of things, unkempt and ragged creatures, with no defense and not a shadow of excuse.

To believe in the risen Lord requires that we live resurrected lives. There is much in the past that haunts us. With the help of Christ we can properly bury those things that haunt us and rise to new life.

Mary Magdalene, the unlikeliest person, was able to say, "I have seen the Lord" (John 20:18). In seeing Him and telling about it, she began to be resurrected, a sign of which she had experienced when

Jesus healed her of seven demons. Thus, Mary Magdalene was an eyewitness to the most important spiritual news of all time. She, along with other women, was last at the cross and first at the tomb. Mary Magdalene was faithful to whom she saw and she told her fellow disciples.

Peace I Leave with You: John 14:27

The early followers of Christ were slow learners. So have been the late followers of Christ. Much of what Jesus attempted to teach was lost on His disciples. They didn't get the point, they argued that what He said would never happen, or they promised more than they ever delivered. It was as if their attention spans were too brief. They never seemed able to stay with Jesus for very long.

The central focus of the New Testament points to the resurrection of Christ as the stackpole around which the followers of Christ gathered. It was the resurrection that finally arrested the attention of the first disciples and provided the cohesion to motivate them to ministry.

There has been a tendency through the centuries to distort the life of Christ and His resurrection by emphasizing either the birth or the death of Christ. Eastern Christianity has emphasized the importance of the incarnation. Because the birth of Jesus has been considered by Eastern Christians as the most significant event in Christianity, the art of Eastern Christianity has provided a variety of manger scenes. Western Christianity has focused on the death of Christ as reflected in the hymnals of Western churches. In the 1975 edition of the *Baptist Hymnal* twenty-eight hymns deal with the death of Jesus while only seventeen seek to proclaim His resurrection. This contributes to the problem of contemporary followers of Christ living on the wrong side of Easter. There is much kinship between the living of those first disciples and that of today's disciples. Their living and ours, if we dare call it living, is carried out behind locked doors.

The first disciples locked the doors because they were afraid (John 20:19). They did not have the assurance of Franklin Delano Roosevelt that "there is nothing to fear but fear itself." What is worse, they did not have faith or hope in the risen Lord. Actually, all they had was the horrible memory of a crucifixion and the rumor of an empty tomb. These two facts were hardly enough to inspire any of them to show their faces in Jerusalem.

Those who were Jesus' disciples were known because they had been seen with Him. They were guilty by association. Part of what locked up the disciples was guilt. Calvary was horridly near. Crucifixion was a dreadful way to die. To have invested three years in ministry, Jesus did not have a great success story according to our standards. He had about one-hundred-and-twenty disciples, but what had they learned? It appears they had learned little. In a time of crisis, when Christ needed them most, what had the twelve apostles done? One had betrayed Him, another had denied any affiliation with Him, and all of them had fled the scene. They might stick their necks out for themselves but not for anyone else, no matter how good He had been for them. They had added to the pain of death for Christ.

The disciples also were afraid because they were insecure. All of them were marked people. If the Jewish leaders were on a witch hunt, some of them in the locked room might be next. The rumor was that the disciples had stolen the body of Jesus. The disciples were near hysteria. They became suspicious. They were acting purely on emotion, thinking about their actions after the fact, if they thought at all. They locked the doors. If the Jewish authorities or the Roman soldiers wanted them, why did they think bolted doors would keep them out?

Fear immobilized those first disciples. Even though Christ had promised them peace, they felt no peace. They either forgot the promise or thought the crucifixion declared null and void all that He had said. Surely no more downhearted and unhappy people could be found the whole world over than this frightened, little group of broken people. They had failed Christ and, as they saw it, He had failed them. The dream that had awakened in them had come to absolutely nothing.

We, too, are locked up by our fears. We are frightened, timid souls. Fear is one of the first emotions we experienced as infants. Our fears were threefold: fear of falling, fear of loud noises or catastrophes, and fear of being abandoned. Similar fears continue to hound us throughout life. As adults we translate the fear of falling into the fear of failing, the fear of losing our places, our jobs, our esteem. Many of us on occasion are frightened by the loud noise of the thought of the death of a spouse, a child, a close friend, the impact of a crippling disease or accident. There is the recurring fear of abandonment. What if our support network evaporates or the springs of our creativity dry up? What if I sit down with pen in hand and discover I have nothing to write?

As I work with people who are in personal crises, I become aware that they often are locked up in fear. Children are dishonest with their parents because they are afraid of parents' reactions. A husband needs to tell his wife about the distance he feels in their relationship but he is afraid of her reaction. A woman refuses a leadership position in the church because she is afraid she won't measure up to the expectations of the congregation.

Probably Margaret expressed what fear is like better than anyone else. Margaret was referred to me by a member of my congregation. She was an attractive woman in her late thirties, mother of two children. She and her husband had separated a year earlier. She had found a full-time job, which had been an agonizing experience because she had never worked away from home. Now she was seeking a better job. Throughout this long year she found herself either crying excessively or on the brink of tears. She entered my office, sat down, and within two minutes diagnosed her situation by saying, "I have a bad case of the what if's and I'm afraid to's." Margaret was locked in fear.

If people get any kind of freedom from their fear bondage, it is more like a resuscitation experience than a resurrection event. We come from the cemetery of buried feelings, bound and gagged by fear. We are fearful, timid souls behind locked doors. We are unsure whether we are trying to keep people in or out, unsure whether we are upholding truth or tradition, unsure whether we are proclaiming resuscitation or resurrection.

Our only hope is for the risen Lord to come through our locked doors and stand among us. Jesus was recognizable and capable of communicating thought after His resurrection although His body appeared and disappeared at will in spite of closed doors. The primary purpose of Jesus' appearances after His resurrection was to establish identity and continuity of the earthly Jesus with the risen Lord. The appearances effected a transition: from the seen to the unseen, from the temporal to the eternal, from the limited to the universal, from the physical to the spiritual. The disciples also were being transformed: from fearful to peaceful, from spectators to witnesses, from powerless to powerful, from vacillating to authoritative.

Christ broke in on those first disciples and sought to dispel their fear, insecurity, and suspicion. After He had passed through the locked doors, Christ breathed on His disciples and began forming them into a new creation, a new kind of existence. Christ offered them a new kind of existence based on resurrection that they might rise up out of their fear into the peace that He offered.

Here we are twenty centuries after the first Easter, with little more than talk about resurrection. We have locked ourselves in fear, immobilized our resources, drawn to ourselves those who agree with us and shut ourselves in. Christ seeks to break in upon us and breathe into us a new kind of existence.

Feed My Sheep: John 21:17

Many characters walk across the stage of the Bible. These characters become real as we discover attitudes, feelings, and events in our lives that correlate with theirs. Naturally, some of the biblical characters have greater appeal to us than others as we learn from them and discover a significant kinship with them. Peter is one with whom many identify closely.

From the recorded events of Peter's life I have the visual image of a crusty old fisherman with a hooked nose, a hunched back, and gray beard. I sense there was a fishy odor that accompanied him. Fishing was in his blood, in a manner of speaking. Peter became a follower of Christ. He wanted so much to say and do the right thing. This characteristic caused Peter to be impetuous and impulsive. He made promises which he did not keep. He was crushed by his guilt. Out of loving forgiveness, Christ restored Peter to full apostleship. The written account of this restoration is recorded in the twenty-first chapter of John, which has instruction for us. We can learn from the dialogue of Jesus and Peter about how love and commitment are related in the lives of followers of Christ.

We in the church engage in an excessive amount of rhetoric. Words often form a proverbial smoke screen used to defend ourselves and behind which we attempt to hide. We speak fluently and passionately about our commitment to God. Impetuously and impulsively we say the correct words with just the right emphasis. Only a brief moment after our lofty promises are made, our stunted actions reveal our hypocrisy. A rooster crows, or some child speaks in his stark honesty about what he sees and hears, and we go limp inside. For the first time or for the thousandth time, the horror of our denial and shallow commitment confront us. We want to hide or run, or we project a calloused, stern appearance, assuring ourselves that we are only human, as if that were excuse enough for any contradiction between our speaking and our living.

Christ's dialogue with Peter is filled with hope. The initial impact of the dialogue is confrontational. I feel the discomfort of Peter as Christ asked him the same question three times: "Simon, son of John, do you love me?" (John 21:15). There seems to be an increasing mixture of feelings in Peter's response, "Yes, Lord, you know I love you" (V. 16). I almost hear Peter saying, "You know I love You, don't You?" Too few days earlier Peter had disclosed the shallowness of his commitment of love and loyalty. The only guarantee that Peter had of his own love for Jesus was his word and Jesus' confidence in his love.

The three questions by Christ and Peter's three affirmations correspond to Peter's threefold denial of Christ. Through this process Peter was forgiven and reinstated to service. Jesus was willing to entrust even His little lambs to one who had completely violated his most sacred oath only a few days earlier. We in the church have failed to learn what Jesus was teaching. There is no sin, no mistake when forgiven that is to keep another from serving God in any capacity. For us to claim that a person is forgiven, and then to deny him the opportunity of serving God through the church is blatant hypocrisy. This denial demonstrates that we have not learned what Peter experienced and what Jesus taught in and through this dialogue between them.

Jesus asked Peter if he loved Him more than these. This is a troubling question, because the grammar does not define who "these" are. Many conclude it refers to the other disciples, but that is so unlike Christ. Christ did not relate to and deal with people by harassing one who had fallen and repented. That often is our way, but not Christ's. Christ did not find an open sore in one's life and rub salt in it. That may be our way, but not Christ's. There is no indication in other situations that Jesus pitted one of His followers against others, and there is even less reason to believe He would do that in the presence of the others. This often may be our approach, but not Christ's.

It seems more likely that Jesus' question about loving Him more than these was a reference to the old life. Earlier in this same chapter of John's Gospel, after two appearances by the resurrected Lord to the disciples, it was Peter who said, "I am going fishing" (V. 3). This was Peter's way of saying in this state of flux and turbulency, I need to feel secure and my security is in doing what I know best—fishing. Thus it was back to the boats for Peter, and several of the others went with him. Peter was back at the old life. He was drawing away from Christ. Perhaps all of Peter's broken promises left a residue of bitter memories, and Peter concluded that Christ no longer wanted him. But it was in the neighborhood of the secure and familiar for Peter, Christ spoke to Peter saying, "You're moving away from Me. That is why I am here" (Author).

Is this not like Christ? He often has broken in on us in the nick of time. We were in jeopardy. We were deciding wrongly. Suddenly some word of His sprang into our minds. Some remembrance of Him rose up and steadied us. And with that we rallied and the crisis safely passed. We are so like Peter. We claim to love Christ, but there are many disclaimers. The discrepancies between our speaking and our living form such a gap that there seems to be no bridge over such a great divide. There are times when we seem to be little more or better than a religious club, run for our interest, propagating ourselves, or, at most, operating for the spiritual profiting of ourselves—just like any other club, a purely self-centered thing. Christ breaks into our midst through someone who is hungry, lonely, or from another religious tradition and says, "Do you love Me?" Are you going to abandon Me? Are you going to desert Me for a few traditions? Are the old ways tugging at you?"

Lip service is insufficient response to Jesus' question, "Do you love Me?" Each time Peter confessed his love, Jesus channeled it with a command to tend and feed the flock of God. The same channeling follows our confessions. Christ is asking for our commitments.

Genuine, significant commitment is tempered with love. When commitment is not undergirded by love, the commitment becomes a duty to keep, an obligation to fill, or an exercise in guilt reduction that is done for relief.

The depth of our genuine love for Christ is revealed in the action we take to shepherd and feed the children of God. All are children of God in terms of needing shepherding and feeding. There is no one we can turn away or determine that we have no reason to love and nuture. It was Christ who brought to light the worth of a person, any person, every person.

We in the church often are guilty of trying to make others in our image. Until they look like us, talk like us, and act like us, they are unacceptable to be loved and nurtured by us. There is a play entitled, *Children of a Lesser God,* which is the story of a speech therapist who meets a woman who can neither hear nor speak. Their love for each other develops. They marry and then spend most of their energy trying to make each other into his or her own image. James is determined to make Sarah talk and Sarah is determined that James will learn to communicate with her in silence. They drive a wedge between each other. The play ends with a hopeful dream and the final covenant in the dream, "I will help you if you will help me." How many of God's children do we drive from the church because we are trying to make them in our image?

The failure of the church to give itself wholeheartedly to the fulfilling of the orders to feed and care for the people, all of the people, seems to be the reason for the church's ineffectiveness and comparative failure in our time. Tiring, personal involvement is not a spectacular event of the church. Yet, to neglect it is disastrous.

The lip service of love for Christ is insufficient. It is life service in the name of Christ that eliminates duty, obligation, and guilt from commitment and tempers it with love. Jesus was saying to Peter, and He is saying to us, that promises of love are demonstrated in and through relationships with others, those who are like us and those unlike us.

The question Jesus asked Peter is repeated daily to us, "Do you love Me?" The authenticity of our affirmative answer is demonstrated in the care and nurture we give to others. Jesus asks, "Do you love Me?" Then He instructs us, "Then love My people, all My people."

Certainly we do not have in the New Testament all of the words Jesus spoke. Actually we have very few of His words for someone who lived thirty-three years, three of which were spent in public ministry. About all we have from Jesus are His stories and illustrations. What public speaker doesn't know, but may hate to admit, that what people remember from his public discourses are the stories? It was true of Jesus as well. Yet mention a mustard seed, a wayward child, a lost coin, a lily of the field, a fig tree, or a tax-collector and Jesus comes to mind. He so captured the essence of life in the everyday events of living that to mention the need of a cup of water is to summarize His invitation to discipleship. With a bath and a meal Jesus demonstrated the needs of all people to commune with God and one another.

Jesus' parabolic life underscored what He said. Because His life and

His words rang true with human experience and need, Jesus' words have become lasting words. The timely and timeless quality of Jesus' words have caused them to be words across time to which people have listened, resisted, argued, debated, and accepted. They are words which have caused people to examine the essence of their lives. His appearances and words following His resurrection punctuated the truth He illustrated in His life and ministry. The words of Jesus are lasting words because they give expression to human encounter with the living, eternal God.

Notes

1. Paul Scherer, *The Word God Sent* (New York: Harper and Row, 1965), p. 189.
2. George A. Buttrick, ed., *The Interpreter's Bible Commentary* (Nashville: Abingdon Press, 1952), Vol. 8, pp. 741-742.

Bibliography

Books

Albright, William Foxwell and David Noel Freedman, eds. *The Anchor Bible.* (Garden City, N.Y.: Doubleday and Company, Inc., 1976), 44 volumes.

Allen, Clifton J. *The Broadman Bible Commentary.* (Nashville: Broadman Press, 1970), 12 volumes.

Barclay, William. *The Daily Study Bible.* (Philadelphia: The Westminster Press, 1958), 17 volumes.

Barclay, William. *The Mind of Jesus.* (New York: Harper and Brothers, 1960).

Beasley-Murray, G. R. *Baptism in the New Testament.* (London: Macmillan and Company, Ltd., 1963).

Buttrick, George A. *The Interpreter's Bible.* (Nashville: Abingdon Press, 1952), 12 vols.

Buttrick, George A. *The Interpreter's Dictionary of the Bible.* (Nashville: Abingdon Press, 1962), 5 vols.

Buttrick, George A. *Jesus Came Preaching.* (Grand Rapids, Mich.: Baker Book House, 1961).

Campbell, Will D. *The Glad River.* (New York: Holt, Rinehart, and Winston, 1982).

Cullman, Oscar. *Baptism in the New Testament,* translated by J.K.S. Reid. (London: SCM Press, Ltd., 1964).

Fant, Clyde E., Jr., and William M. Pinson, Jr. *20 Centuries of Great Preaching.* (Waco, Tex.: Word Books, 1971), 13 vols.

Glenn, C. Leslie. *A Scornful Wonder.* (New York: David McKay Company, Inc., 1977).

Harris, Thomas A. *I'm OK—You're OK.* (New York: Harper and Row, 1967).

Hinson, E. Glenn. *The Reaffirmation of Prayer.* (Nashville: Broadman Press, 1979).

Kittel, Gerhard and Gerhard Friedrich, eds. *Theological Dictionary of the New Testament.* (Grand Rapids: William B. Eerdmans Publishing Company, 1964), 10 vols.

Lidz, Theodore. *The Person.* (New York: Basic Books, Inc., 1968).

Marney, Carlyle. *He Became Like Us.* (Nashville: Abingdon Press, 1964).

Moody, Dale. *Spirit of the Living God.* (Philadelphia: The Westminster Press, 1968).

Peck, M. Scott. *People of the Lie, The Hope for Healing Human Evil.* (New York: Simon and Schuster, 1983).

Pfeiffer, Charles F. *Baker's Bible Atlas.* (Grand Rapids, Mich: Baker Book House, 1961).

Robertson, A.T. *Word Pictures in the New Testament.* (Nashville: Sunday School Board of the SBC, 1930-33), 6 vols.

Scherer, Paul. *The Word God Sent.* (New York: Harper and Row, 1965).

Segler, Franklin M. *Christian Worship: Its Theology and Practice.* (Nashville: Broadman Press, 1967).

Smith, Charles W. F. *The Paradox of Jesus in the Gospels.* Philadelphia: The Westminster Press, 1969).

Stagg, Evelyn and Frank. *Women in the World of Jesus.* (Philadelphia: The Westminster Press, 1978).

Tournier, Paul. *A Place for You.* (New York: Harper and Row, 1968).

Willimon, William H. *Worship as Pastoral Care.* (Nashville: Abingdon Press, 1979).

Yeager, Randolph O. *The Renaissance New Testament.* (Bowling Green: Renaissance Press, Inc., 1976), 14 vols.

Periodicals

Hinson, E. Glenn. *The Review and Expositor.* (Berne, Ind.: Economy Printing Concern, Inc., Winter 1980), Vol. LXXVII, No. 1.

Hinson, E. Glenn, ed. *The Review and Expositor.* (Louisville: The Southern Baptist Theological Seminary, 1972). Article by Frank Stagg, "Salvation in Synoptic Tradition," Vol. LXIX, No. 3, pp. 355-367.

Stagg, Frank. "Salvation in Synoptic Tradition," *The Review and*

Expositor. (Louisville: The Southern Baptist Theological Seminary, 1972). Vol. LXIX, No. 3, pp. 355-367.

Sermons

Claypool, John R. "The Power Problem," Broadway Baptist Church, Fort Worth, July 14, 1973, Vol. XII, No. 24.

Stookey, Laurence H. "Remember Your Baptism," Unpublished sermon, August 6, 1975, Wesley Theological Seminary, Washington, D.C.